A Harvest Saved

Francis O'Neill
and Irish Music in Chicago

A HARVEST SAVED

FRANCIS O'NEILL
AND IRISH MUSIC IN CHICAGO

NICHOLAS CAROLAN

OSSIAN PUBLICATIONS

I gcuimhne Bhreandáin Bhreathnaigh

Published by
Ossian Publications
14/15 Berners Street, London W1T 3LJ, UK

Exclusive Distributors:
Contact us:
Hal Leonard
7777 West Bluemound Road Milwaukee, WI 53213
Email: info@halleonard.com

In Europe, contact:
Hal Leonard Europe Limited
42 Wigmore Street
Marylebone, London, W1U 2RY
Email: info@halleonardeurope.com

In Australia, contact:
Hal Leonard Australia Pty. Ltd.
4 Lentara Court, Cheltenham,
Victoria, 3192 Australia
Email: info@halleonard.com.au

Order No. OMB132
ISBN 978-1-900428-11-8

Picture research by Nicholas Carolan
Front cover illustration of Francis O'Neill by Einion Rees
Cover photos of Chicago c. 1900 and Francis O'Neill 1904
courtesy of Chicago Historical Society
Layout and design by Pier Kuipers

Visit Hal Leonard Online at
www.halleonard.com

Contents

	Page
Introduction	3
Part 1 Beginnings	5
Part 2 Police Life	13
Part 3 Private Life	23
Part 4 Musical Life	29
Part 5 Legacy	55
Appendix Books by Francis O'Neill	62
Notes	66
Information Sources	74
Acknowledgments	78
Index	79

Francis O'Neill

A Harvest Saved:
Francis O'Neill
and Irish Music in Chicago

Daniel Francis O'Neill (1848-1936) of Cork and Chicago is an outstanding figure of the Irish diaspora. From a rural background in Ireland he rose by native ability to become chief of police in the second largest city in the United States, and, after an early life that belongs to the novels of Conrad and London, he made in middle age the largest collection of Irish traditional music ever published. A traditional musician himself from childhood, he has had through his publications the greatest single personal influence on the course of Irish traditional dance music in this century.

Of all the collectors of Irish music, Francis O'Neill has told us most about his own life and collecting work. Interviews he gave to journalists and biographers in Chicago, his own studies of Irish music, surviving letters and other sources detail his Co. Cork youth, his coming to America and his involvement with other traditional musicians there.

Roġa an τaoiseaiġ ui niall.   CHIEF O'NEILL'S FAVORITE.

Cronin.

1556

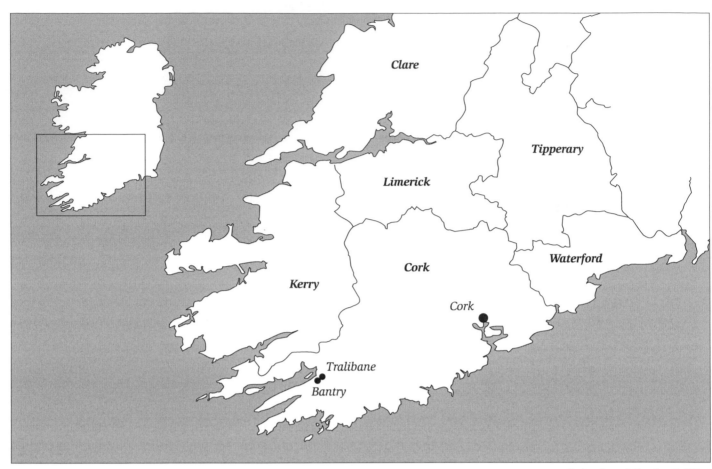

Ireland and the South-West

Tralibane

1 BEGINNINGS

The O'Neill House in Tralibane 1996

Below: 'Feb. 1847... The Sketch is taken on the road, at Cahera, of a famished boy and girl turning up the ground to seek for a potato to appease their hunger... Not far from the spot... six dead bodies had lain for twelve days, without the least chance of interment...'
Below right: Hornpipe named for O'Neill's mother

Francis O'Neill's immediate ancestors, O'Neills and O'Mahonys, were members of long-established septs of these families in west Munster. His maternal grandparents, Donal O'Mahony or *An Cianach Mór* (c. 1777-1857), 'a latter-day chieftain',[1] and Mary O'Mahony *Cianach* (c. 1779-1857), kept open house for travelling musicians near Drimoleague in the wild and remote glens of west Cork during the first half of the nineteenth century. His mother Catherine or Kit[2] (c. 1812-1900),[3] raised in this musical atmosphere, later transmitted to her own children, by her lilting and singing as she worked around the house, the melodies she had memorised there. His father John (c. 1801-1867), a well-to-do and educated farmer[4] from the nearby townland of Tralibane,[5] three miles west of the coastal town of Bantry and some twelve miles south of the Co. Kerry border, had a house and land in an ancient valley marked with standing stones, near the banks of the Owenashingane, a tributary of the river Ilen. He too was a singer of songs, in Irish and English, after the daily routine of farm work was over.[6] O'Neill's sisters were also singers,[7] and one, Nancy, was married to Jerry Daly, a renowned local dancer.[8]

Francis O'Neill, christened Daniel[9] and familiarly known as Frank, was born in Tralibane on 28 August 1848,[10] the youngest of seven children.[11]

Although he was born during the Great Famine, the ravages of which were becoming less severe at the time of his birth, O'Neill would have had no personal memories of it. His native parish of Caheragh in the Union of Skibbereen, part of an intensively potato-growing region, was catastrophically affected by the potato blight. Corpses of those who had died from hunger and fever floated down the Ilen, and Skibbereen became a byword for famine throughout Ireland and beyond. The starving children at Caheragh in James Mahoney's famous 1847 sketches for *The Illustrated London News* were O'Neill's contemporaries, and he may have known them, if they survived.[12] O'Neill however makes no personal allusion to the Famine in his voluminous writings, and only occasional passing references to its effects on music in the country in general.

Bantry and its hinterland seems to have recovered quickly from the worst effects of the Famine, and O'Neill's formative years were

CRANNCIUIL CAIT NI MACÁAṁNA.   KIT O'MAHONY'S HORNPIPE.

F.O'Neill.

1593

5

Bantry in the 1860s

spent in a period in which agricultural activity increased and the area began to open up to tourism and trade. As elsewhere in Ireland however, the population of the countryside continued to decline through emigration, much of it to the United States.[13] Constitutional nationalism, of the kind espoused in Westminster by O'Neill's older contemporaries, the Bantry politicians and writers A.M. and T.D. Sullivan, was strongly supported in the area from the 1850s, but Fenianism was also widespread there late in the decade and in the 1860s: Jeremiah O'Donovan Rossa worked in the town during O'Neill's childhood.[14]

Music, song and dance were an integral part of the largely Irish-speaking rural society in which O'Neill grew up,[15] and his father's

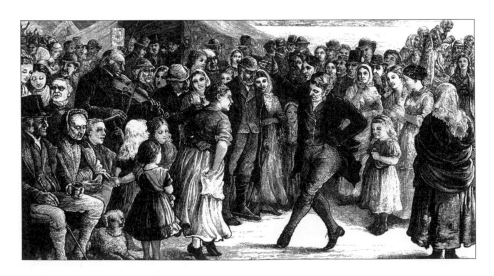

Outdoor music and dance in Gougane Barra, West Cork, near Tralibane, early 1870s

Cork piper 1852

Verses on the Píobaire Bán by a schoolmate of O'Neill's

DEAR OLD COLLOMANE.

When I was but a boy and played upon the village green,
Where you could hear the bagpipes in happy days I ween,
The boys and girls .would often go to hear the Piper Bawn,
And many a pleasant day I spent in dear old Collomane.

From Aughaville we often went on Sunday afternoon
To hear old Peter play the pipes—he gave us many a tune;
His wife sat close beside him as gentle as a fawn
And told them take their partners in dear old Collomane.

Irish flute player 1853

house and that of a sister were venues for neighbourhood dances. Pipers, fiddle players and flute players were frequently heard at cross-road dances in summer and at farmhouse dances in winter. The parish supported two professional pipers in the years after the Famine: Charley Murphy, or 'Cormac na bPaidreacha', who had a regular outdoor pitch at Tralibane Bridge, a few hundred yards from the O'Neill home, and Peter Hagerty, 'An Píobaire Bán', who played at the nearby Colomane crossroads.[16] The latter made an indelible impression on the young O'Neill:

> With what wonder and curiosity we youngsters gazed on this musical wizard, as he disjointed his drones and regulators and tested the reeds and quills with his lips... Being young and insignificant I was put to bed, out of the way, while the others went to enjoy the dance next door. It just chanced that the piper was seated close to the partition wall... Half asleep and awake the music hummed in my ears for hours, and the memory of the tunes is still vivid after the lapse of fifty years.[17]

Traditional songs in Irish and English and traditional dance tunes played on fiddle, flute and uilleann pipes were the staple musical fare of the locality, but popular national songs such as 'The Croppy Boy' and 'The Rising of the Moon' were also known,[18] and there was a temperance marching band in Bantry town.[19]

Inheriting his mother's gifts of 'a keen ear, a retentive memory, and an intensive love of the haunting melodies'[20] of the race, the young O'Neill began learning music on the flute from a neighbouring gentleman farmer, Timothy Downing (c. 1806-82).[21] By then the simple-system wooden flute had been for some decades coming into the hands of traditional musicians, after it had fallen out of favour among the better-off performers of classical and popular music who had first played it in Ireland. It may still have had an aura of its more privileged beginnings, and it was an instrument rarely played by professional traditional musicians. O'Neill's teacher owned a large collection of music in manuscript, but he does not seem to have taught his pupil to read music, a skill that O'Neill acquired to some degree years later in America.[22]

While he heard the Irish language commonly about him as he grew up in the bilingual society of Tralibane, and probably spoke it as a child,[23] it would seem that O'Neill was raised in English, as was common for people of his class in the second half of the nineteenth century. English was certainly the only language of the relatively new national school system within which he received his formal education, and it was the language of many of his father's songs. Years later in America, he was a keen supporter of the Gaelic League from its foundation in the 1890s and took the trouble to arrange the translation of thousands of tune titles into Irish for publication, even having special tools manufactured to cut a Gaelic typefont.[24] He organised an evening of traditional music for Dr Douglas Hyde, president of the Gaelic League and future president of Ireland, during Hyde's visit to Chicago in 1906,[25] and is recorded as having chatted in Irish with Hyde.[26] O'Neill himself said that 'while I speak and read Irish I have not attempted

Irish manuscript. Therefore I must rely on the "Bearla".[27] His library, one of the largest Irish collections in North America, as late as 1919 seems to have contained none of the League's publications,[28] and it is probable that he never acquired more than a rudimentary reading ability in the language. His last book, in 1924,[29] was dedicated to the spirit of the Gaelic League, and his work in music should be seen in the context of the League's regenerative efforts in language and national culture.

Tune titles in Irish from O'Neill's 1903 collection

As a child, the talented O'Neill was both physically daring and studious, and this mixture in his nature is seen throughout his life. After beginning his formal education at the nearby Dromore national school,[30] he moved on to the larger national school in Bantry.[31] Continuing wild and restless in Bantry, O'Neill was at the same time outstanding in his knowledge of Latin, Greek[32] and mathematics, and was nicknamed 'Philosopher' by a teacher.[33] He became a monitor in the school at fourteen, and then a teacher there, but left home at the age of sixteen,[34] seemingly running away after a disagreement with an older brother who had been appropriating his salary for successful investments in cattle.[35] A desire to see the world and travel the seas he glimpsed from Bantry Bay doubtless also motivated him, and a contributory factor may have been the recent suppression of music and dancing in the Tralibane area by a new parish priest.[36] Going to Cork City, some sixty miles away, with letters of introduction to Bishop Delaney, O'Neill had almost fulfilled his parents' and teachers' hopes for him by enrolling in a seminary to become a priest or a Christian Brother, when he changed his mind and embarked instead on a life of travel and adventure.[37]

Bantry Bay from the Tralibane Road

The white building beside the church housed the national school which O'Neill attended. It was demolished about 1896.

In March 1865 O'Neill worked his passage by boat to Sunderland in the north of England and there signed on as a cabin boy under a Captain Watson,[38] sailing during the following years to Russia, Egypt, the United States, the West Indies, Mexico, South America, Hawaii, and Japan, and rounding the Cape of Good Hope. The effects on him of moving from the sheltered and homogeneous society of Tralibane to mixing with a hundred nationalities in the ports of the world can only be imagined, but it clearly made him tough and self-reliant. On his first voyage to the United States, on the steamship *Emerald Isle* in August 1866,[39] he met with Anna Rogers, a young emigrant from Feakle, Co. Clare,[40] and his future wife. About 1867, the year his father died, O'Neill interrupted his voyages to return home, but left again after a few months.[41] Almost forty years would pass before he would next see Ireland.

British vessel of 1865. O'Neill sailed in a variety of sailing ships and steamships on the high seas and on the Great Lakes.

Having been picked up by ship's lifeboat after falling overboard and fracturing his skull on a trip to Odessa,[42] he was ship-wrecked on Baker's Island,[43] a coral island in the mid-Pacific, while serving before the mast on the *Minnehaha* of Boston. Rescued with his fellow crewmen in a near-starving condition by a passing brig, and brought first to Honolulu and then to San Francisco, O'Neill became one of the almost half a million Irish immigrants who entered the United States in the 1860s.[44]

After a period as a shepherd at the foot of the Sierra Nevada mountains, where he herded flocks of up to 3,000 sheep,[45] and a further stint at sea during which he rounded Cape Horn,[46] he left the sea permanently, having sailed around the globe before his twenty-first birthday. He settled down temporarily in Edina, in Knox County, Missouri, where he qualified as a teacher and began work in the winter of 1869. Restless again, he moved to Chicago in 1870, at the age of twenty-two, to become a sailor on the Great Lakes. In the autumn of the year at Bloomington, Illinois, he married Anna Rogers, with whom he had kept in contact.[47] She also was a lover of music from an area where traditional music was strong, and at their wedding party O'Neill is said to have sung 'Bímís ag Ól', a favourite song of his father's.[48] In 1871 he

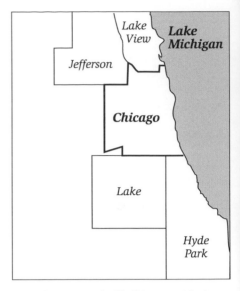

returned permanently to Chicago to work first as a labourer in the freight house of the Chicago and Alton Railroad[49] and then as a lumber yard supervisor, before joining the police force in July 1873.[50]

Chicago, which had been incorporated as late as 1837, was then a bustling frontier city, crowded with a heterogeneous population of immigrants – Germans, Scandinavians and Irish chiefly – and rebuilding itself after it had been largely burned down in October 1871, in the most disastrous fire in American history. Its position on the edge of Lake Michigan, the largest lake in the United States, and of the sweeping western plains gave it the character of a port, a cattle town and trading post. As the terminus of a canal linking the Mississippi with the Great Lakes, and the centre of the transcontinental railway system, it quickly became the commercial hub of the Middle West, with a concentration on grain and meat. Great wealth, evidenced in the magnificent buildings which were beginning a new American tradition in architecture, existed side by side with extremes of want in crowded ghettos. Violence and anarchy were in the air, especially in the nationally notorious Levee red-light district, but by 1890 Chicago had grown to be to the second-largest city in the United States. In his years in Chicago, O'Neill lived through periods of break-neck economic devel-

United States and old Chicago with the surrounding townships which were incorporated in the city in 1889

Below left: Rebuilding Chicago after the Great Fire of 1871. O'Neill had come to Chicago before the Fire, but his time there was essentially in the period of reconstruction and expansion.
Below: Music was commonly part of the community activities of the Chicago Irish.

ANNUAL

PICNIC

AND

DEMONSTRATION·

Given by the

Ancient Order of Hibernians

OF COOK COUNTY

Saturday, July 15,'05

AFTERNOON AND EVENING

at Brand's Park
California, Belmont and Elston Avenues

IRISH GAMES AND SPORTS .. IRISH MUSIC

Prominent Speakers Will Make Addresses

MUSIC BY VALLELY ORCHESTRA

Tickets, 25 Cents Each

ALL NORTH AND WEST SIDE CARS TRANSFER TO GROUNDS

opment, which were often followed by severe depressions and labour troubles, and witnessed such momentous episodes there as the World's Columbian Exposition of 1893, the gangland wars that followed the introduction of Prohibition in the 1920s, and the Great Depression of the 1930s.

The Irish had been settling in the Chicago region since the 1830s when they had come to dig the Illinois and Michigan Canal. The majority of these early settlers were from Co. Cork.[51] By the time of the O'Neills' arrival in the early 1870s, the Irish-born in Chicago numbered some 40,000 and formed 13% of the total population of the city. They were politically influential beyond their numbers, especially at local level, and were the dominant element in the Chicago Democratic party by the 1880s.[52] The superior employment opportunities available in the Midwest and a more muted anti-Irish nativism there enabled them to move more quickly into the skilled working and lower middle classes than their more numerous compatriots in the eastern cities, and they mixed freely with other nationalities.[53] During the period of O'Neill's music collecting activity in the city, the numbers of Irish-born rose as high as 75,000, and with the inclusion of their American-born children there was a peak of over 235,000 Irish in Chicago by 1900, again some 13% of the local population.[54]

Above and below: Examples of notable architecture in O'Neill's Chicago: the Chicago Board of Trade and one of several gigantic department stores

MARSHALL FIELD & CO.'S RETAIL STORE, CHICAGO

Above and in detail: Chicago policeman on the beat, Maxwell Street, c. 1900 Left: Dial of a Chicago police alarm-box of the 1880s: a selection of the crimes O'Neill met on the street. The alarm system was introduced by police chief Doyle and city electrician Barrett.

2 POLICE LIFE

Chicago police make an arrest in the 1890s

At the time Francis O'Neill enlisted in the Chicago police, it was a small force of about 550 men, many Irish among them, struggling with crime, prostitution and political corruption on a grand scale.[55] As in all the centres of Irish settlement in the United States, Irishmen in Chicago saw policing as a natural route of advancement from labouring and other menial work, one which combined adventure with security. It was a route which posed difficulties in Ireland, but not in America, as O'Neill himself pointed out:

> It is surprising how many fine musicians are to be found among the Irish constabulary who, owing to the peculiar conditions and sentiments heretofore existing in Ireland, were doomed… to waste their sweetness on the desert air of the barrack room. In America… all officers of the law are citizens and voters and reside with their families promiscuously in the community and are rather looked up to than otherwise… Being neither constables nor employees of an unpopular government, the American police are peace officers of the State and Municipality and therefore men of standing in the commonwealth.[56]

The force in Chicago has always had a strong Irish component, its position protected by the political influence of the Democratic Party. The police occupied a difficult position among the many power blocks in the city. Fraught relations between organised labour and organised capital led to regular armed clashes during O'Neill's decades as a police

Attack on Chicago police patrol-wagon by striking workers, 1886

officer. The Haymarket anarchist riots of 1886, in which seven policemen were killed by a bomb, and the Pullman railroad riots of 1894,
during which federal troops were called in, were only two of the
serious disturbances which occurred in O'Neill's time. In labour con-
flicts police sympathies were generally with the strikers but their duties
lay with the employers and public order. At times of severe hardship,
on the other hand, the city's police stations were used to house the
homeless.

O'Neill's initial posting was to Harrison Street Station in the
business district of Chicago.[57] During his first month on the force, in
August 1873, he was shot in an encounter with John Bridges, a notorious burglar, and thereafter carried a bullet encysted near his spine.[58] For
his bravery he received instant advancement to patrolman. Although
ambitious, he was spikily honest, and uncooperative in doing favours
for local ward politicians,[59] and was said once to have 'whaled an alder-
man'.[60] He was eventually moved from Harrison Street for being 'too
busy' and 'too good'.[61] By degrees he built a reputation for efficiency,
courage and energetic determination, and in spite of disgruntled politicians gained regular promotion, a rise aided by his secretarial skills and
his successes in the new competitive police examinations.[62] He became
desk sergeant in Deering Street in 1878, an Irish neighbourhood where
traditional musicians and singers were 'delightfully numerous',[63] a
member of the general superintendent or chief of police's office in

*One of several 1873 newspaper reports of
the shooting of O'Neill*

*Personnel of Deering Street Police Station
in 1872, six years before O'Neill came
there as a desk sergeant. Several officers
here were presumably his colleagues, and
they may include some of the officers he
played music with in the station.*

O'Neill after his appointment as Captain, 1894

1884, and patrol sergeant in 1887, in which year it was noted that he had never been fined, suspended or reprimanded.[64]

O'Neill was made lieutenant in 1890, private secretary to the general superintendent in 1893, and captain in 1894 when he achieved first place in the captaincy examinations.[65] As captain he was in charge of the Eighth District which included the infamous Chicago Stockyards. He had to face down a large force of strikers there during the vicious Pullman railroad riots, and his chief of police Michael Brennan made special mention of him in his annual report for 1894:

> The most serious affray of the strike occurred on the afternoon of July 7th at 49th and Loomis streets. A crowd of several thousand people had gathered... There were hootings by the crowd at the soldiers, and some stones were thrown and shots fired. The state military first charged the crowd with bayonets and afterward fired several volleys, resulting in the killing or fatally wounding of four men and the wounding of some twenty. After the military fired they... returned to the city. The crowd became more threatening, and Capt. Frank O'Neill, with a force of police officers, charged the crowd and completely dispersed it.[66]

O'Neill finally became general superintendent, or chief, himself on 30 April 1901,[67] commanding from Room 127 in City Hall, with an annual salary of $6,000.[68] His unimpeachable reputation as a serving police-man, his high standard of education, and his ability to creditably represent the city on public occasions, were reasons given by the mayor's office for O'Neill's appointment,[69] and he was described by the local Irish press as a man of 'clear mind, independent character, broad education, and thorough integrity'.[70] Clearly he was also brought in to

Militiamen fire into the crowd at Loomis and Forty-ninth Streets: the July 1894 affray in which O'Neill earned commendation

Newspaper portrait of O'Neill on the day of his appointment

O'NEILL WIELDS BATON OF CHIEF.

New Police Head Moves to the City Hall and Receives Congratulations.

IS CALLED "CAP'N" STILL.

Talks Over Plans with the Mayor and Is Expected to Shift Some Officers.

GLAD HAND BRIGADE CALLS.

Newspaper announcement of O'Neill's appointment

The new Chief. This appears to be a doctored version of one of O'Neill's photos as a captain.

City Hall, Chicago, where O'Neill had his office

reform the police department,[71] but said that only 'loafers' among the police had reason to fear him: 'I hate loafers... and unfortunately there are a number on the Chicago police force'.[72] He described himself as 'the Mayor's hired man' and dryly commented that 'I suppose I shall have a lot of friends now. That is customary, and I shall not be surprised at their number'.[73]

With an annual budget of some $3,500,000 and a force of 3,300 men under his control – some 2,000 of them said to be Irish[74] – he was an able administrator, responsible for the policing of a population of almost two million people in a territory of almost 200 square miles[75] in the most violent of American cities. He was a strict disciplinarian, driving corrupt detectives off the force,[76] stamping out abuses among

O'Neill moves against police corruption, August 1901. Detectives were removed from office or later retired.

CHIEF OF DETECTIVES LUKE P. COLLERAN, STAR WITNESS IN YESTERDAY'S SESSION OF POLICE INVESTIGATION.

"THERE IS NO FAVORITISM SHOWN IN THE DEPARTMENT!"

"NO SIR! I KNEW NOTHING ABOUT THE LARKIN PAPERS!"

"YOU TAKE THAT FEATHERSTONE MATTER! THAT IS AN OUTRAGE!"

"I AM NOT RESPONSIBLE FOR ANYTHING THAT HAS BEEN DONE WITHOUT MY SIGNATURE"

"MY OFFICE HAS A RECORD!"

CHIEF O'NEILL TESTIFIES

O'NEILL AS A WITNESS.

The testimony given by Superintendent O'Neill before the Civil Service commission on Tuesday contrasted pleasingly with that given by other witnesses. His testimony was not, like that of Lieutenant Joyce, a series of vehement negatives. It was not interspersed, like that of Officers Tracy and Cramer, with refusals to answer lest he should incriminate himself. It was a plain story, quite calculated to convince the commission and the public.

The Superintendent's statement was a summary of the confessions made to him by Officers Tracy and Cramer. These two men, acting under the advice of lawyers, withheld, when on the stand, the interesting part of their confessions, but nobody doubts that they told the Superintendent exactly what he says they did. It would have been more to their credit if they had

'Eat a Pork Chop and Be Happy': fast food and an Irish saloon on the Levee, Chicago's red-light district, in the 1890s. The Levee was a continual problem for O'Neill and other Chicago police chiefs.

the police generally, curbing their involvement in party politics, and revising their Book of Rules.[77] He struck interviewers as energetic and resolute:

> In his office at the City Hall when visited in regard to anything pertaining to police affairs Chief O'Neill is aggressive, short, quick, with a policeman's bluntness... He rapidly decides what is right... and he cannot be moved from his position'.[78]

O'Neill cracked down on prostitution and gambling, and tried also to hold the legal line against the powerful Chicago meat-packing companies during the Stockyards strike of 1902 by ordering their security

O'Neill testifying at Iroquois Theatre fire inquest 1904

feaḋóir an ṁeara ḣarrison.   MAYOR HARRISON'S FEDORA.

799

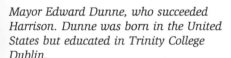

Mayor Carter Harrison Jnr with his trade-mark brown fedora, and a reel named in his honour

Mayor Edward Dunne, who succeeded Harrison. Dunne was born in the United States but educated in Trinity College Dublin.

guards to be arrested for carrying concealed weapons.[79] Although his work was now largely administrative, he did occasionally leave his desk to visit his men on the streets or participate in raids. In December 1903 almost 600 people died in Chicago's most disastrous fire, in the Iroquois Theatre, and O'Neill was active there:

> Chief of Police O'Neill and Assistant Chief Schuettler, after ordering the captains and men from a dozen stations to go to the fire, themselves rushed to the theatre and led the rescuers into the building. At the doors the dead were piled eight or ten feet high…[80]

O'Neill was twice re-appointed general superintendent under successive administrations, in 1903 and 1905, his third appointment being under a new mayor, 'an unheard-of proceeding in American municipal politics'.[81]

In spite of his successes, O'Neill eventually realised that he would be unable to reform the police force to his own standards: 'Every man knows how to manage a woman until he gets married. I had some of those ideas myself until I got to be chief, and then, like the man who gets married, I found out'.[82] Edward Dunne, the new mayor who came to office in 1905, belonged to a faction of the Chicago Democratic Party opposed to O'Neill's patron Harrison. O'Neill actually tendered his resignation to Dunne early in 1905, but it was not accepted until a Teamsters' transport strike, which had convulsed Chicago in the first half of the year and which O'Neill had been handling to the satisfaction of the business community, was brought to an end.[83] Demoralised by the deaths of his children, and out of sympathy with Dunne's administration, Chief O'Neill, as he was generally known,[84] left this highest office in July 1905,[85] at the age of fifty-seven, after more than thirty-two years of continuous police service.

That O'Neill was an outstanding public official is clear from the spontaneous cheers that greeted his appointment,[86] his distinction of serving as chief under two rival political administrations, and the almost universal chorus of approval that his conduct of office received.[87] Even Joseph Kipley, the chief of police who was removed from office to make way for him, had a high opinion of O'Neill.[88] His political master, Mayor Carter Harrison Junior, was slightly less enthusiastic, finding him a 'conscientious, industrious, if not brilliant chief'.[89] There are indications too that he was a humane officer, understanding of the economic pressures that drove some to crime.[90] The first black policeman in the United States to be promoted above the rank of patrolman was appointed by O'Neill.[91] The famous Russian anarchist Emma Goldman, arrested and at first illegally interrogated by the police in

Left: O'Neill on his retirement in 1905: 'Then I was wan and worn... full of official nervewrecking responsibilities...'
Below: The most sincere testimonial: a newspaper report of 1901

MORE THIEVES QUIT CITY.

PICKPOCKETS ARE GLAD TO ESCAPE CHIEF O'NEILL.

Three Dangerous Men Take a Train for New York, Sorrowfully Declaring as They Leave That the "Graft" Is "Tough" Under the New Police Regulations—Superintendent Makes Another Tour of the Levee and Sees Improvement.

New York's plaint that Chicago thieves are invading the East because of the activity of Chief of Police O'Neill was further justified yesterday when three of the most expert pickpockets in the West boarded a train for the Eastern metropolis. Those men, " Ed " Jacobs, " Sam " Scopek, and " Ollie " Scott, said a sad good-by to an escort of detectives as a Nickel Plate train started on its run out of the city.

The three pickpockets were arrested by Detectives Rohan and Morgan of the Central Station. When they were brought up before Lieutenant Rohan they begged to be let go, promising they would leave the city at once. They were arraigned before Justice Prindeville, however, and each of them was fined $10 and costs.

The prisoners again pleaded for release, and finally the police agreed to let the men go if they would leave Chicago at once. Justice Prindeville suspended the fines and the prisoners were escorted to a ticket office, where they bought transportation for New York. As they were put on board the Nickel Plate train at 5 o'clock Jacobs said:

"This town is too tough a graft, now. I don't want any of Chicago in mine while O'Neill is Chief of Police. Good-by."

Chief Sees the Levee.

Meanwhile Chief O'Neill paid another visit to the levee yesterday and found conditions improved. There still were things which called for treatment by Inspector Hartnett, he said, but " some of the surface evils had been rubbed off."

"I have sources of information regarding affairs in the levee," declared the Chief. " As fast as things are called to my attention I send an order to the Harrison Street Police Station and the matters are attended to."

In the afternoon the police raided the house of Jet Kelly at 429 Clark street, directly across the street from St. Peter's Church. Complaint had been made to Captain Mahoney by members of the church that the women of the resort were overbold. Later the police raided the house at 76 Van Buren street, said to be conducted by Dora Linke. In all twelve arrests were made.

O'Neill Has a Dyspepsia Cure.

Dyspepsia, Chief O'Neill says, afflicts many members of the police force, and he lays the blame for the malady on the " dog watch " system. By this system a policeman is detailed to go out and watch for fires and other trouble at 4 o'clock in the morning. He wanders about the district until 8 o'clock in the morning. Then he is relieved, but must return to work at noon. In the four hours off duty the policeman has to take breakfast and his noonday meal, and the crowding together of these meals is what gives him dyspepsia, the Chief says.

The Chief proposes to substitute the " 11 o'clock system." By this method the policeman works from 11 o'clock in the morning

Chicago in 1901 on unfounded charges of complicity in the assassination of President McKinley, records her gratitude to O'Neill, who ensured that she was particularly well treated and not extradited to New York without evidence.[92] An enquiry into corruption in the police force during O'Neill's tenure found no cause against him, but was rather sympathetic that he was not given adequate resources by the municipality for his task.[93] It is accepted by modern historians of the Chicago police that he was one of the few general superintendents to be personally untainted by corruption,[94] and his patent honesty shines from every page of his writings. Even as late as 1920, it was written of him that 'he vindicated every pledge of his office, made safe the bulwarks of life and property in Chicago, and struck more terror into the heart of the criminal than any man who has ever filled this position'.[95]

It is sometimes jokingly said that O'Neill neglected his police duties for music and undermined the Chicago police force by packing it with Irish musicians, but, as will already be clear, this is far from the truth. He frequently put aside music under the pressure of his official

'City Hall as a Literary Center': O'Neill shown among the literary men who worked there. His prose style was much admired.

Bernard Delaney of Offaly

duties, and only the first of his eight books was produced while he was still a policeman. Even this one took over a dozen years to bring to publication. The force naturally had many Irish traditional players within its ranks, even before O'Neill himself joined,[96] and while he did often sponsor the employment of others, as he tells us himself, it was not to any very disproportionate degree. Once however he went as far as New York to enlist an outstanding piper in the force:

> … there came to Chicago, Power's delightful Irish play The Ivy Leaf. Their piper… took sick and… passed away… To take his place temporarily, [Bernard] Delaney reluctantly consented; but such were his success and popularity, that Powers insisted on keeping him permanently on an increased salary… Nothing but a more desirable position in Chicago could be expected to allure him to return. When that had been arranged for, the writer intercepted The Ivy Leaf company in New York city and returned to the western metropolis, accompanied by our piper, where he became and still is a member of the Chicago police force.[97]

In general however O'Neill's musical activity was confined to his home and to the homes of his friends, although music did occasionally intrude on his official concerns:

One Monday morning I unexpectedly encountered John McFadden in the corridor outside my office in City Hall, and wondering what could have happened since we parted the evening before, I asked, 'What brings you here so early, John?' 'I wanted to see you privately in your office, Chief', he quietly replied. To my suggestion that we could transact our business just as well where we were as in my office, where so many were waiting, he did not agree, so in we went through three intervening rooms. When the door was closed behind us Mac did not keep me long in suspense. 'Chief, I lost the third part of 'Paddy in London' which you gave me last night… when I got up this morning, all I could remember were the first and second parts, and I want you to whistle the missing part for me again'.[98]

John McFadden of Mayo, an oral composer and fiddle player with a large repertory and great powers of variation: 'The airy style of his playing, the clear crispness of his tones, and the rhythmic swing of his tunes, left nothing to be desired…'

On another occasion, his unexplained absence from City Hall on a visit to his music amanuensis and fellow-policeman Sergeant James O'Neill gave some humourist an opportunity to start a rumour which Francis himself reports:

While [I was] contentedly scanning the evening newspapers in the parlor, happy in the freedom of the moment, in through the kitchen rushed a policeman with bulging eyes to announce that 'the Chief was assassinated'. This was news to me, but I didn't believe it. With a look of terror he precipitately backed out on seeing me, convinced that it was my ghost which appeared to him, and it was with difficulty he told the Sergeant the outlines of the alleged tragedy.[99]

Below and below left: From a newspaper account of O'Neill's supposed assassination. This drew public attention to his musical activities: the newspaper artist imagines Francis and James O'Neill playing music. They presumably supplied the music notation which is the air of a song Francis learned from his parents.

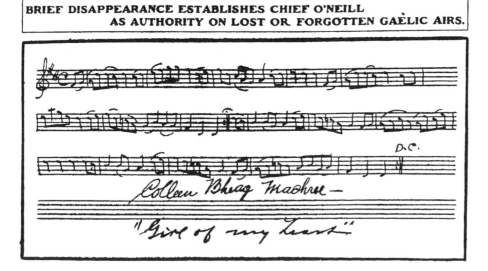

3 PRIVATE LIFE

Although he was sometimes criticised by others in the Irish community for jeopardising his dignity by mixing with disreputable and even criminal musicians,[100] O'Neill's 'strong-mindedness and sense of self'[101] enabled him to follow his principles and disregard such criticism. In print he held somewhat dogmatic and censorious opinions to which he returned time and time again, but which were relieved by an observant sardonic sense of humour and an eye for the absurd. The aggressive and blunt character of O'Neill the policeman was not seen in his private life. A writer of 1897 said of him that

> In his manner he is unassuming, even to a degree of shyness... Never obtrusive with his own opinions, he is under all circumstances a courteous and obliging gentleman tolerant of the prejudices of others... In religion he is a Roman Catholic but of that most liberal type which offers the entirest freedom to others... in appearance [he is] a man of medium height... of robust constitution, great strength and splendid endurance... possessed of a keen business instinct... Though Captain O'Neill has always been classed as a Democrat, his vote has been given independent of political party distinctions...[102]

While O'Neill does not seem to have taken a very active part in party affairs, he was by 1902 a valued member of the local Democratic Party of Cook County. Its published history displays his portrait almost as prominently as that of Chicago's Mayor Harrison, who first appointed O'Neill to office.[103] Edward Dunne, Harrison's successor as mayor, who re-appointed O'Neill, was also a Democrat. Although O'Neill's position made him prominent in the Irish life of Chicago, he was not identified with the leading Irish organisations there.[104] But he only partly became Americanised. He was described as having a 'strong sympathy with the cause of his native land',[105] and attended Irish Fellowship Club dinners in Chicago.[106] He was also a supporter of Home Rule, making a generous subscription to the Irish Parliamentary Party Fund when John Redmond visited Chicago in 1904.[107] The landscape of his private imagination was the country where he had spent the first sixteen years of his life, not the one in which he spent the next seventy.

Humorously describing himself in 1916, O'Neill said 'you must know I'm hardly companionable myself. I can't smoke, I dislike intoxicating liquor, neither am I political or an agitator.'[108] Although he directed all his efforts towards the protection of old traditions and was scathing towards those who jettisoned them, at the same time he had

Some of O'Neill's surviving phonograph cylinders in University College Cork

a broadminded welcome for progress and innovation. He increased his writing output by dictating some of his music commentaries to a stenographer for typing,[109] was an early user of the phonograph to record musicians in Chicago,[110] kept up with new Irish 78s issued during the 1920s[111] and was later a keen listener to Irish music on radio.[112] He was an admirer of the Irish composer Victor Herbert who had achieved success in the field of popular music in America.[113] As he said himself in reference to music:

> I see no good reason why everything should be condemned or dis-
> credited except that which is known to be ancient.[114]

O'Neill also had a sharp business sense, and became independently wealthy by investing his savings in real estate, the Chicago pastime.[115] After spending the early years of their married life in Popular Avenue in the central city, the O'Neills moved in the 1880s to a large suburban house in Hyde Park,[116] following a trend of the decade among the successful Chicago Irish.[117]

O'Neill's youthful experience of the clerical suppression of music in Caheragh parish 'by a gloomy puritanical pastor'[118] marked him deeply, and it was a subject he returned to again and again in his published writings and letters. The piper Peter Bán Hagerty, whose music had entranced O'Neill as a child, ended his life in the workhouse after dances of all kinds were forbidden by the local parish priest, and many Irish musicians O'Neill met in America had similar stories to tell. History repeated itself in the 1890s in Tralibane when O'Neill's own nephews also experienced clerical suppression of music there, and he felt that such actions impoverished rural life and made it monotonous:

> As usual emigration was the only relief from such intolerable con-
> ditions, and a depopulated Ireland is the result.[119]

O'Neill could also be acerbic about Catholic church power among the

Fr James K. Fielding of Kilkenny, a flute player and Gaelic League activist who was a fellow-musician and friend of O'Neill in Chicago

O'Neill's last son Rogers, and a lament composed for him

Irish in the United States, but he was by no means anti-clerical and he considered many priests his friends, especially those who were musicians. He said of the priests he criticised:

> It was really the parvenu, and not the wellborn, who indulged his inflated sense of importance in such autocratic ways. I number many clergymen among my relatives in this generation, and it is my honour to entertain clergymen in my home even now.[120]

The dualities noticed in O'Neill in youth have their counterparts in the adult O'Neill. Apollonian in his public role of enforcing the rule of law and in his private collecting and ordering of music, he was also drawn to the dionysian: heroism in riots, property speculation, and the very practice of music itself. A leading figure in the public life of Chicago and a tireless activist among its Irish musicians, he simultaneously pursued his private obsessions of study and creation. His unusual combination of practical and reflective abilities, and his job, enabled him to span several separate and very different worlds, including those of the Irish Americans stereotyped as 'lace-curtain' and 'shanty'. Most importantly, his talents and experiences made it possible for him to connect the oral music of Ireland with the universal literate-music tradition for its preservation and dissemination.

The O'Neills had ten children, five sons and five daughters.[121] One daughter[122] and all the sons died young. Three of the boys died in childhood, on the same day, from diphtheria,[123] and the last and oldest, Rogers, a promising college student and violinist, died at the age of eighteen of spinal meningitis in 1904.[124] These deaths cast a gloom on the family and on O'Neill from which he never fully recovered. In deference to his wife's feelings, he no longer played music in the house after 1904 and stored his cylinder sound recordings and cylinder player in the home of a friend.[125] Referring in 1916 to the convivial Irish-born family of his sister Nancy and Jerry Daly who also lived in Chicago, O'Neill said 'my family, all American-born and graduates… were all (and are yet, those who are living) friendly and kindly, but… we were always beastly sober, so where was the fun in visiting us…?'[126] Mirroring the common experience of middle-class Irish-American women at the turn of the century,[127] two of the surviving O'Neill daugh-

25

John Smithwick Wayland

Alfred Perceval Graves

Michael Flanagan of Kildare, a military schoolmaster and Oriental scholar who contributed biographical information on Irish musicians to O'Neill's publications

ters, Julia and Caroline, married, and two, Anna and Mary (May), who did not marry, became schoolteachers.[128]

In the summer of 1906, the year after his retirement, O'Neill made his first journey home to Ireland for almost forty years, and also went to Wales. With his wife, he visited relatives and friends in Cork and Clare and traditional musicians around Ireland, with many of whom he later kept up a correspondence. His six-week trip through Munster and Leinster[129] included a visit to the recently founded Cork Pipers' Club where he was delighted to meet pipers old and young,[130] and was especially impressed by its founder John Smithwick Wayland. He also raised monuments to his maternal grandparents and parents in Co. Cork,[131] acted as an adjudicator in the instrumental competitions at Feis na Mumhan in Cork City,[132] attended Gaelic League functions in Dublin, and collected music in Clare.[133] In Wales, having travelled from Dublin to Holyhead in the company of the writer and folksong enthusiast A.P. Graves,[134] he visited the son of Timothy Downing, his flute teacher of half a century earlier, to examine Downing's music manuscripts. He was associated during his Irish trip with a group of some 80 Irish Americans, practical patriots mainly from Chicago, who had come to Ireland, on Douglas Hyde's suggestion, to enquire into the industrial and educational conditions of Irish life with a view to improving them.[135]

Monument to his grandparents erected by O'Neill in Co. Cork in 1906

Although he had many pleasant musical experiences in Ireland, especially in Clare,[136] O'Neill was not generally impressed with the state of music there, and felt it to be inferior to what might commonly be heard in Chicago.[137] In his references to the trip a disillusioned note appears which is heard increasingly in his writings. He came eventually to feel that the Irish at home and in the United States were turning their backs on Irish music:

> Few of our people care a snap for... Irish music. The poor scrub
> who graduated from the pick and shovel and the mother who for

ERIN'S SONS AT A PICNIC.

CHICAGO'S IRISH PEOPLE MAKE MERRY IN A GROVE.

Ancient Order of Hibernians Has Its Annual Outing—Women Join in the Athletic Contests and Visitors Recall Memories of Land Across the Ocean—Two United After Forty-five Years—Reels and Clogs Danced by the Older Persons.

Irish men and women of Chicago made merry at Gardner's grove yesterday, dancing to tunes brought across the sea and dear to the Celtic heart. It was the annual picnic of the Ancient Order of Hibernians of Cook county, and the attendance was large, although threatening weather kept many from the grounds at One Hundred and Twenty-third street and Michigan avenue.

While the older visitors danced the old Irish reels and clogs, the younger persons danced to the more modern music.

Newspaper report of 1903 showing generational changes in musical taste among the Chicago Irish

many years toiled in some Yankee kitchen will have nothing less for Katie and Gladis or Jimmy or Raymond but the very latest agony, if you please. Time and again have I been disgusted by the tittering and mockery of Irish audiences when a piper strikes up a merry tune and this disconcerting conduct comes not from the American born but from the Irish born mainly.[138]

He felt too that the Irish in general lacked 'calm deliberation, dispassionate analysis, and tenacity of purpose',[139] and saw it as a serious defect in the Irish character both in Ireland and America that they were

always glorifying the legendary and historical past, and leaving to the future the realization of their dreams. The present – the only time within the compass of our energies – gives us but slight concern as long as our leaders dope us with vainglorious praise and holiday oratory.[140]

This feeling of disillusion was reinforced by disagreements and jealousies among the Chicago musicians that came to a head after his return to America, and by what O'Neill considered the ungrateful behaviour of some musicians he had helped, especially that of his brother-in-law, the outstanding piper Bernard or Barney Delaney,[141] for whom he had arranged a position on the police force. His preference for musicians like his colleague James O'Neill, 'talented, but not temperamental'[142] was not very often satisfied. In addition, the number of

O'Neill in the 1930s when he was in his eighties

traditional musicians in the United States was declining with the 20th-century decline in Irish emigration there, and the older generation of musicians who were O'Neill's contemporaries were not being replaced as they died. Eventually however, obeying 'some impulse akin to instinct',[143] he overcame his disillusionment and resumed work on his preoccupation.

The remainder of O'Neill's 'long and adventurous life'[144] – he lived to be eighty-seven – was devoted to his musical and antiquarian[145] researches and writings, to the building up of his library which became one of the largest collections of Hiberniana in North America, to an extensive correspondence with other Irish music enthusiasts in his distinctive calligraphy, to his 80-acre farm at Palos, Illinois,[146] and to 'Glengariff', his winter home on the Gulf of Mexico at Ocean Springs, Mississippi, where he fished and spent time with his family.[147] He also collected plate, pottery and photographs.[148] Anna O'Neill died in 1934, and grieved by her death he was looked after by his daughters. His interest in Irish music continued until the end of his life. Still corresponding on his favourite topic of uilleann piping in 1935, he said of his health that 'quietness, and freedom from worry and excitement, is the price of life.'[149]

Francis O'Neill died of heart failure on 28 January 1936 in his home at 5448 Drexel Avenue,[150] in the fashionable Hyde Park area, where he had lived for almost fifty years.[151] He was buried in the family mausoleum in the mostly Irish Mount Olivet Cemetery in Chicago.[152] Obituaries appeared in various American and Irish publications, almost all copied from an extensive obituary in a Chicago newspaper.[153] He was survived by his four daughters, a number of grandchildren, and other relatives. His voice, strong and Americanised but still recognisably Irish, remains on cylinder recordings he had sent back to Ireland, appropriately introducing music played by the Chicago musicians.[154]

O'Neill family mausoleum in Chicago

O'NEILL, FORMER CHIEF OF POLICE, MUSICIAN, DIES

Leading Authority on Folk Tunes of Ireland.

Francis O'Neill, who was chief of the Chicago police force from 1901 to 1905, and was known as one of the greatest modern authorities on Irish folk tunes, died yesterday in his home at 5448 Drexel boulevard. He was 87 years old.

Mr. O'Neill had been in ill health since the death of his wife, Anna, 18 months ago, and had been confined to bed since Christmas. Death was attributed to a heart ailment.

Born near Bantry in Cork county, Ireland, Mr. O'Neill had an adventurous youth. He was cabin boy and sailor on vessels engaged in Mediterranean and Black sea trade for several years, and sailed around the Horn to New York, circumnavigating the globe from 1866 to 1869. He joined the Chicago police force in 1873, and remained in the department 32 years until his retirement in 1905.

FRANCIS O'NEILL.

Wounded by Burglar.

A month after Mr. O'Neill joined the force he was shot in the back by a burglar, whom he captured. He carried the bullet in his body the rest of his life. He became a sergeant in 1887, a lieutenant in 1890, and a captain in 1894.

He was named chief of police [the title then was general superintendent] by Mayor Carter Harrison in 1901, and was reappointed twice, serving until July 25, 1905, when he went into retirement. From then on he devoted himself to the study of Irish music and wrote seven books on the subject, collecting the lyrics and detailing the picturesque traditions surrounding them.

4 MUSICAL LIFE

Only known photograph of O'Neill as a musician

In all his wanderings and throughout his police career and long retirement, O'Neill was obsessed with music, 'music mad'[155] as he said of himself. He continued with his childhood instrument the flute as his main instrument, and privately considered himself 'a fair freehand fluter'[156]. At different times he played the fiddle[157], the Scottish Lowland pipes[158] and Scottish Highland pipes on which he described himself as 'a tasty performer'.[159] He was also 'an excellent performer on the [uilleann] pipes', according to his friend the Rev. Dr Richard Henebry, professor of Celtic at the University of Washington D.C.[160] The enthusiastic Henebry is likely to have been the anonymous admirer of O'Neill's piping made fun of by the piping historian Séamus Ó Casaide:

> Captain O'Neill is a musician himself, and a good one. He has at least one admirer who places him above all the musicians of the world. If Paderewski were to give one of his masterly performances of a Mozart sonata, or if Kubelik were to play the Hungarian Rhapsody with that wonderful artistic feeling which is so characteristic of his work, and if one were to say to a certain distinguished votary of music, 'Isn't that exquisite?', the chances are a hundred to one that the reply would be, 'Ah, yes, but you should hear Chief O'Neill play "The Foxchase"!'[161]

O'Neill was also a singer like his father and mother[162], and is said to have been able to whistle 'beautifully'.[163] In later life he confined himself for an instrument to the tin whistle.[164] Although he seems not to have been a dancer, it is unlikely that he could have grown up in Tralibane without some participation in the social dancing which took place in the family home. Certainly he had a lively interest in the history of traditional dancing, and a thorough understanding of the interconnections between dancing and the dance music which was his speciality.

O'Neill's playing of the flute for a Kanaka sailor after his rescue from shipwreck in the Pacific saved him from the malnutrition that affected his fellow crew members:

> Rations were necessarily limited almost to starvation. One of the Kanakas had a fine flute, on which he played a simple one strain hymn with conscious pride almost every evening. Of course, this chance to show what could be done on the instrument was not to be overlooked. The result was most gratifying. As in the case of the Arkansas traveler, there was nothing too good for me. My

dusky brother musician cheerfully shared his 'poi' and canned salmon with me thereafter. When we arrived at Honolulu, the capital of the Hawaiian Islands, after a voyage of thirty-four days, all but three of the castaways were sent to the Marine Hospital. I was one of the robust ones, thanks to my musical friend...[165]

At the age of nineteen O'Neill was picking up new tunes in the San Joaquin Valley in California. In Missouri, he learned music from Thomas Broderick, a flute player from Galway and a school director in Edina with whom he boarded. Settling into his new world there, he attended dances to acquire tunes and was already exhibiting his life-long habit of naming untitled tunes after the people or occasions with which he associated them:

> Not a week passed during the winter months without a dance or two being held among the farmers. Such a motley crowd – fiddlers galore, and each with his instrument. Irish, Germans, French – types of their respective races – and the gigantic Kentuckians, whose heads were endangered by the low ceilings... Seated behind the fiddler, intent on picking up the tunes, was my accustomed post... tunes distinctly obtrude on my memory, viz... a quickstep, which I named 'Nolan the Soldier'. Nolan had been a fifer in the Confederate army during the Civil War. His son was an excellent drummer, and both gave free exhibitions of their skill on the public square at Edina to enliven the evenings...[166]

Chicago proved a treasurehouse of Irish music for O'Neill in the 1870s and the following decades, and provided him with an opportunity for learning about the spectrum of traditional music that would not have been available to anyone in Ireland. Living within its 200 square miles were musicians from all the thirty-two counties of Ireland and many American-born musicians of Irish descent, and a stream of visiting Irish professional musicians, especially pipers, was constantly passing through the city. The post-Famine demoralisation that affected music so badly in Ireland had far less effect in Irish America, where performers and audiences shared a relatively lively scene. Nevertheless active enthusiasts for traditional music formed only a minority of the Irish immigrant community, as in Ireland itself, and the opinion-makers of the community, while paying lip-service on public occasions to the ethereal glories of Irish music, generally considered jigs, reels, horn-pipes, street ballads and country songs vulgar, and songs in Irish irrelevant to their new lives. The musical interests of most Irish in America seemed centred more in American popular music, Irish nationalist songs, or the *Irish Melodies* of Thomas Moore. Nevertheless there was

Thomas F. Kerrigan from Longford, a professional piper who briefly kept a music saloon in Chicago in 1873

Irish Pipers' Club
San Francisco

Group of Irish musicians in San Fransisco which was broken up by the earthquake of 1906. Their music, like that of similar groups in the American cities, has gone unrecorded.

a dormant and sometimes shamefaced hankering after traditional music among many Irish-Americans which occasionally manifested itself in public.[167] Thronged dancehalls, music saloons and vaudeville theatres enabled some musicians to earn a living from traditional music, and were also the laboratories in which a distinct form of Irish-American music evolved in the late nineteenth century. New York, Philadelphia, Boston, and other centres of Irish settlement also had their musicians and singers and instrument makers, but not, unfortunately, their Francis O'Neill. His arrival in Chicago was timely: the experience he gained and the work he carried out in music during his first four or five decades there could not have been duplicated much earlier and certainly not later. By the 1920s demographic and cultural changes among the Chicago Irish would almost have swept away their older traditional culture.

O'Neill was soon making the acquaintance of the Chicago players and memorising their tunes. The musicians constituted a loose social network:

> Among Irish and Scotch music lovers, every new arrival having musical taste or talent is welcomed and introduced to the "Craft"… and there is as much rejoicing on the discovery of a new expert as there is among astronomers on the announcement of a new asteroid or comet.[168]

In the police force he also met with many fellow-musicians adapting their music to their new American circumstances:

> Many an impromptu concert in which the writer took part enlivened the old Deering Street Police Station about this time. A unique substitute for a drum was operated by Patrolman Michael Keating, who, forcing a broom-handle held rigidly against the maple floor at a certain angle, gave a passable imitation of a kettle drum... a charming fluter was Patrolman Patrick O'Mahony, commonly known as 'Big Pat'... Born in West Clare, his repertory of rare tunes was astonishing, the 'swing' of his execution was perfect, but instead of 'beating time' with his foot on the floor like most musicians he was never so much at ease as when seated in a chair tilted back against a wall, while both feet swung rhythmically like a double pendulum.[169]

At least once in Deering Street he was able to combine police duty and personal pleasure:

> The strains of a slashing but unfamiliar reel floating out on the night air from the lowered windows of Finucane's Hall caught my eager ear one Saturday night, when Tommy Owens was playing for a party. Being on duty as Desk Sergeant at the time, and as the police station was just across the street, I had little difficulty in memorizing the tune. Although it had never been printed it soon gained wide circulation among experts, and it had become such a favorite with Inspector John D. Shea, that it has since been identified with his name.[170]

'The Ladies' Pantalettes' was the older name for Shea's favourite reel.

Even on patrol O'Neill kept an ear open for music:

> While [I was] travelling on post, one summer evening in 1875, the strains of a fiddle coming through the shutters of an old dilapidated building on Cologne street attracted my attention. The musician was an old man named Dillon, who lived alone, and whom I had seen daily wielding a long-handled shovel on the streets. His only solace in his solitary life besides his 'dhudeen' was 'Jenny', as he affectionately called his fiddle. A most captivating jig memorised from his playing I named 'Old Man Dillon' in his honor.[171]

George West, a Chicago-born helper in a blacksmith's shop, aged 17 in 1901, after he had been discovered by O'Neill in the Stockyards district. O'Neill considered him a phenomenal fiddle player, especially of jigs, and had high hopes of him. 'Work, however, was not for his taste...' and eventually 'an incident in his life rendered a trip to the far West advisable'.

And in the midst of a busy professional life when he was rising to the top of the police hierarchy he still pursued his interest single-mindedly:

> One evening I accompanied him [George West, a fiddle player and criminal from the Canaryville slum district of Chicago] to make the acquaintance of his friend O'Malley, who eked out a living by playing at house dances. A trip through a few dark passageways and up a rickety back stairs led us to his apartments. There was a welcome for West, but his introduction of me as a Captain of Police was very coldly received. With evident reluctance, O'Malley produced the fiddle, on West's request, while his wife and children viewed me as an interloper, with unconcealed misgiving. Calling the children to me in a friendly way, and giving them some coin, effected a sudden change in the atmosphere. Beer soon appeared on the table, and under its mollifying influence all indications of suspicion and distrust quickly disappeared.[172]

When the great Columbian Exposition was attracting world-wide attention to Chicago in 1893, O'Neill's focus was the uilleann piping and music anecdotes of Turlough McSweeney, the famous Donegal musician who had been brought over to Chicago to play at the Irish exhibition.[173]

Turlough McSweeney of Donegal, probably photographed in Chicago in 1893

Contact with such a wide assortment of musicians deepened O'Neill's understanding of Irish music and its various regional traditions, and added greatly to the store of music he had carried in his memory from his native Cork. At the same time he was reading everything he could find about Irish music, and had standing orders with booksellers in America, Britain and Ireland for relevant publications. His mind teemed with music, and tunes had distinct personalities for him. In the midst of a music session, he was the musician who could not only make the normal personal connections between tunes in oral circulation, but who also had an understanding of their chronology and distribution on the basis of their printed history.

O'Neill also circulated among Scottish Highland pipers in Chicago to learn their music, and was judge of the Highland piping competitions of the United Scottish Societies at their annual picnics for seven consecutive years.[174] Through the Scottish musicians, he met in the early 1880s[175] a musician, a namesake but no relation, who would eventually be an essential collaborator in the work of preserving Irish music for which he is now remembered.

James O'Neill, born in 1863[176] and some fifteen years Francis's junior, at the time of their first meeting was living near the Deering Street Police Station and working as a stoker in the Bridgeport pumping works.[177] In his spare time he was gaining a reputation as an accomplished fiddle player. A quiet and unassuming native of County Down who had lived also in Belfast, James had a large store of Ulster melodies which he had learned from his father, a fiddle player and compiler of Irish music manuscripts. He also had a wide familiarity with Scottish music and was a composer. Francis used his influence to enable James to join the police force where he eventually rose to the rank of sergeant. James O'Neill had what Francis lacked, the ability to note down tunes quickly and accurately from the playing and singing of others.[178]

James O'Neill as a young policeman

Sometime in the later 1880s[179] when he had had long acquaintance with the musicians of Chicago, Francis O'Neill began to realise that there was yet much Irish traditional music to be collected and preserved that had escaped earlier collectors. He recruited James O'Neill to the project of collection and started to visit him regularly at his home in Brighton Park so that the tunes remembered from Francis's childhood in Cork could be noted down from his dictation in a private manuscript collection. Some of the early Tralibane tunes were vividly present in his mind, others barely remained on the edge of memory:

> 'The Proposal', or 'He Asked Me to Name the Day' is an air of much beauty when sung or played with expression. Forgotten since early youth, it came to me like a flash one afternoon. For fear of again losing it I grasped Sergt. O'Neill's bow-hand, lest his strains unhinge my memory. This unpublished melody, which possesses marked individuality, came dangerously near passing into oblivion.[180]

William Walsh of Galway, one of the Highland pipers with whom O'Neill was friendly in Chicago and a source of tunes

As months and years passed and word of their enterprise spread, others contributed tunes to the collection and James O'Neill began visiting musicians in their homes to note their music. Sleeping memories were stirred and tunes not heard for generations began to be recalled:

> On a recent occasion, to the astonishment and delight of a score of Irish musicians who prided themselves on their comprehensive knowledge of their country's music, a violinist who left his native valley over forty years ago played dozens of excellent tunes, then heard for the first time by his audience. And this was but one of many similar instances.[181]

Manuscript and printed collections were contributed by well-wishers, and winnowed for undiscovered pieces. One musician ingratiated himself with musicians who were withholding tunes so that he could

Edward Cronin of Tipperary, a weaver, machinist and composer who was one of O'Neill's chief sources in Chicago: 'he would play on for hours at a time such tunes as memory presented, his features while so engaged remaining as set and impassive as the sphinx... it was his open boast that he never forgot nor forgave an injury...'

Rev. Dr Richard Henebry of Waterford, fiddle player, early Irish ethnomusicologist, professor of Celtic at Georgetown University, Washington D.C., around 1900, when he knew O'Neill, and professor of Irish at University College Cork from 1909. He is said to have suggested the term 'Sinn Féin' to Arthur Griffith. A keen supporter of O'Neill in the early years of their acquaintance, he cut the connection because of an imagined slight.

learn them and pass them on to the collectors. Another who could write music noted his own tunes as well as those of others. Sisters and wives added to the store from their childhood recollections. Some melodies were jotted down when overheard in barber shops, on trolley cars and at railway crossings,[182] others had a most convoluted history of acquisition:

> When Mr Gillan [of Longford and Chicago]... visited his boyhood home, he learned of a celebrated violinist, Mr Kennedy, who lived on a farm a short distance from Ballinamore, County Leitrim. No. 46 ['Katie's Fancy'] caught Mr Gillan's fancy, and while writing the tune, Mr Kennedy told him, that being in town one day he heard a travelling flute player play it on the streets of Ballinamore. He followed him up for some time hoping to learn the tune, but as the flute player frequently changed his numbers, Mr Gillan [*recte* Kennedy] was obliged to visit his lodgings that night and pay 4 pence for the manuscript of it to the flute player. Mr Gillan praised this tune very highly, and when he returned to Chicago he was not at all inclined to be liberal, and only as a special favour to his particular friends would he allow Miss Nellie to play it for them on the piano. One day while [I was] engaged in a pleasant chat with Mr Gillan, whose daughter did not share her father's sentiments, she slipped up stairs, copied the tune and quietly gave it to me. When I got home with my precious document, I contrived to commit the tune to memory, and whistled and played it for others until the tune is now pretty well known in Chicago.[183]

Irish-language and Irish Ireland enthusiasts belonging to the accelerating Gaelic Revival of the 1890s, such as the Rev. Dr Henebry, were regular visitors to the various homes, including that of Francis O'Neill, where the Chicago musicians met. Henebry was loud in O'Neill's praises:

> It mattered not the source, he was ever alert, and can truly give testimony that he has rescued many a melody from lips that were soon afterwards sealed in death. Amongst the most prized of his great collection is a parcel of about four hundred airs that his mother used to sing. In thus forestalling the undertaker and rescuing those priceless gems from oblivion, Mr O'Neill has rendered services of incalculable value to the cause of Irish nationhood... He has ever been a staunch friend to Irish musicians, and brought to light many an unconditioned custodian of our music... He pro-

Interior of the Chicago Auditorium

moted informal meetings of pipers and fiddlers at his own house, and encouraged players from all parts of Ireland by his generous patronage, and taught his children to play his music in the Irish way. A foretaste of the fruits of his labours was given at the [Chicago] Auditorium meetings, where 3,000 people were moved to ecstasy at the thrill of their own music... But a full fruition of the pleasure that Chicago players can afford was accorded me by the privilege of an invitation to a pipers' meeting held at Mr O'Neill's. The full assemblage was present, and almost every class of music was performed as ever before in Ireland. I was astonished at the wonderful proficiency of the players and the inexhaustible extent of their repertoire... I know nothing in art so grand, so thrilling as the irresistible vigor and mighty on-rush of some reels they played... And some of the older song-airs revealed, with sob and sigh, a kind of secrets that may not be spoken for very fear.[184]

Douglas Hyde, president of the Gaelic League, in 1906, the year he met O'Neill in Chicago. The quality of the musical entertainment provided for Hyde in the Auditorium at an official reception for him on 11 January so disgusted O'Neill and his friends that they invited him to a proper musical reception the following night.

Clearly by this time the activities of the Gaelic League in general and of O'Neill and his friends in particular had changed perceptions of traditional instrumental music among the organisers of formal Irish functions in Chicago. Where once this music would have been seen as belonging only to the saloon and dancehall, and the old world of poverty which so many Irish were trying to leave behind, it was now finding a sanctioned place among classical musicians on the concert platform, and audiences were being allowed to follow their tastes in publicly enjoying it. At a monster rally in the Central Music Hall in 1901 to honour the memory of Robert Emmet, O'Neill's presentation was the most popular:

Prof. F.H. Edelman's selected overture was greatly applauded, as was also the magnificent singing of the 'Tom Moore Quartette', the artists being D.J. Malvern, George H. Killand, Miss Betty O'Brien and Mrs. Dr. Sheppers. The singing and playing of Prof. R.J. McGuirk were the admiration of the house, and he was enthusiastically encored. Prof. Simon J. Forhan recited 'The Battle of

Glendalough' in fine style, and Miss Mary Dorgan gave a Gaelic recitation which was well received. The ancient Irish music rendered by Capt. Frank O'Neill's Modern Irish Bards, Messrs. James O'Neill (who was accompanied by Miss E.W.L. O'Neill), Barney Delaney, Adam Tobin, James Early and John McFadden set the audience wild with enthusiasm.[185]

Although in all of the collecting activity Francis O'Neill was the driving force and the final arbiter, he was careful to give due credit to James and to his many other collaborators, such as the fiddle players John McFadden from Mayo and Edward Cronin from Tipperary, flute player Fr James K. Fielding of Kilkenny, and pipers James Early of Leitrim, the outstanding Patsy Touhey of Galway, and Barney Delaney of Offaly, his brother-in-law, whom he regarded as the finest piper he had ever heard. These were all performers of outstanding musicality, the kind who would have been important local music figures had they remained in Ireland or who might have made a national name for themselves had they flourished in the 78 recording era of 1920s New York. In Chicago, by the 1890s, they had absorbed large repertories from a wider musical acquaintance than they would have had in Ireland, and were ripe for recruitment to a great project by the purposeful and influential O'Neill. He had a particularly high regard for Patsy Touhey, a professional entertainer and recording artist, both as a person and as a musician, and persuaded him to reveal some of the secrets of his art in print.[186]

His scrupulous efforts to be just in his printed attributions of tune sources led O'Neill into trouble with his musicians, as pieces he

Below left: John McFadden of Mayo and Sergeant James Early of Leitrim (right), a regular duet in Chicago and important sources for O'Neill. Early supplied O'Neill with tunes from an older generation of his family, the opening bars of which he had noted in a memorandum book. 'Kindly, unassuming, patient, tolerant, helpful, and hospitable', Early reeded chanters for pipers from all over America. Below right: Patrick J. Touhey of Galway, the leading professional piper in O'Neill's America, who picked up and disseminated music in all the Irish communities there, and for whom O'Neill had a high regard: 'the genial, obliging and unaffected wizard of the Irish pipes.'

IRISH MUSIC CLUB, CHICAGO.

Father W. K. Dollard.   Ed. Cronin.   Rogers F. O'Neill.   Francis O'Neill.   Timothy Dillon.   John McFadden.   Michael Kissane.   James Kennedy.
John McElligott.   M. G. Enright.   John Duffy.   John Ennis.   Chas. O'Gallagher.   Wm. McCormick.   Michael Dunlap.   Thos. Dunphy.   Father J. K. Feilding.
John Conners.   Barney Delaney.   John K. Beatty.   Tom Ennis.   James Early.   James Cahill.   Adam Tobin.
Garrett J. Stack.   James Kerwin.

Far left: Bernard or Barney Delaney of Offaly, O'Neill's brother-in-law, for whom he found a position on the police force, and whom he considered the finest piper of his acquaintance: 'music was in him and it early found expression... his style was truely the dancers' delight.. unconcerned and self-possessed under all circumstances in public or private, he plays on undisturbed...' O'Neill did not find Delaney very obliging as a man or as a musician, but many of his published versions do come from him. After retiring from Chicago to the southern states, Delaney spent some time in Cuba.
Left: The Hanafin brothers of Kerry and Boston, William and Michael (right), multi-instrumentalists and dancers, whom O'Neill met in 1905 in Boston, and whose musical history he noted. Michael recorded commercially in the 1920s.

Turlough Carolan, the blind 18th-century harper-composer, whose music was a focus of O'Neill's antiquarian researches. In 1903 he published 75 tunes attributed to Carolan, some of which he had received from oral tradition.

A number of O'Neill's informants lived in Ireland and their music came to him directly or indirectly, especially for his later collections. Mrs Bridget Kenny, a street player in Dublin, was credited by him as a source, her music having been recorded by an enthusiast and transmitted to O'Neill.

collected from and ascribed to one might have been learned by the contributor from another member of the group.[187] He and his collaborators found the richest area for collection to be the Brighton Park locality, west of the Stockyards; South Chicago, while home to many Irish people, was the most barren.[188] In 1907 he listed forty-five players, including himself,[189] who were the chief sources of his collections.[190] Forty were men, five women. All but four were Irish-born: six from west Cork; four each from Clare, Kerry, and Leitrim; three each from Kilkenny and Mayo; two each from Down, Galway, Kildare, Limerick and Tipperary; and one each from Antrim, Cavan, Dublin, Longford, Offaly, Tyrone and Waterford. These figures do not of course indicate the proportions of county or regional music in the collections, but they do suggest that there were areas of Irish tradition, such as those of Donegal and Sligo for example, which O'Neill could only have lightly touched upon.

About 1901 the informal sessions of the Chicago musicians were regulated by the establishment of an 'Irish Music Club'[191], and the holding of monthly meetings in a rented hall. O'Neill was president.[192] Picnics and balls were organised and the musicians were paid from the proceeds, a course of which O'Neill approved:

> What drives our poor musicians into drunkards' graves? False conception of hospitality – Money denied them, but drink forced on them.[193]

Following an initial period of success, disputes among the club managers about office and money caused the best musicians to drift away and

> After less than eight years of inharmonious existence, the most enjoyable, companionable and representative association of Irish musicians, singers and dancers ever organised in America degenerated into a mere shadow of its former prominence...[194]

He himself eventually cut his connection with the Club:

> Personally I've been through the mill, and nothing but the prestige of rank and authority enabled me in one instance to prevent a probable tragedy at a special meeting of the officials... Fortunately news of this incident did not reach the press, and having narrowly escaped a serious scandal, I never attended another meeting.[195]

By 1912 O'Neill could say that not even a remnant of the Club remained and that few of the former members were on speaking terms.[196]

Although he was one of the fraternity of musicians, O'Neill seems to have been able to stay above the quarrels, and seems to have been held in high regard by all:

The Irish musicians of Chicago and vicinity... assembled Wednesday evening, May 22 [1901], at the residence of Mr James Kirwan... The occasion was a reception to Frank O'Neill, whose unremitting and self-sacrificing labor in the revival of Irish music places him pre-eminently the leader in that particular field in America today. No leader in any cause ever received a more spontaneous and hearty welcome than was accorded Chief O'Neill... The assembled musicians and their friends filled the spacious rooms and parlors to overflowing, and the Chief, a proverbially modest man, was visibly overcome... His face was radiant with happiness, as if the scene around him was the culmination of all his labors on behalf of Irish music, for here and there among the crowd he observed his collaborators in the arduous and patriotic task he had set himself of compiling a book of Irish music that will be in quantity and quality be superior to... any others extant.'[197]

O'Neill's elevation to police chief in April 1901 reflected glory on his fellow musicians and was celebrated by them.

Musical tributes were also paid to O'Neill at other times: Edward Cronin composed 'Caroline O'Neill's Hornpipe' for one of his baby daughters, for instance, and a hornpipe 'Rogers O'Neill' for his son; and a lament 'Rogers O'Neill' was composed after Rogers' death in 1904, although its composer is not known.[198] After O'Neill's death Tadhg O'Crowley of Cork published a warpipe march of his own composition 'Captain Francis O'Neill'.[199]

John Ennis of Kildare, piper and flute player, and his Chicago-born son Tom, fiddle player and piper. A policeman and sometime journalist, John Ennis became president of the Irish Music Club after O'Neill's resignation. Tom Ennis moved to New York as a professional piper, where he started one of the first Irish-American record companies and recorded commercially in the 1910s and 1920s.

When more than 2,000 tunes had been recorded in manuscript, a general desire had developed to have them printed. It was decided that a popular work would be produced which would also contain tunes in common circulation, previously printed music from rare collections, Moore's *Melodies,* and modern Irish popular compositions. Some of James O'Neill's compositions were also to be included. It was also decided to print two and even three settings of the same tune if they each had merit.

An advisory committee was set up to sit in judgement on tunes to be published and decide on the best versions. The members, in addition to Francis and James O'Neill, were Early, Delaney, McFadden, Cronin, and Patrolman John Ennis from Kildare, a flute player and piper. Disagreements immediately arose and one opinionated and domineering member silenced the rest.[200] The committee only met once.[201] The two O'Neills continued alone, persisting in spite of the demands of police work which saw them working all day and sometimes all night. Among their difficulties was the problem of being sure that duplicate tunes in different keys or with different names were not included:

> … it required great caution, aided by an acute ear and a retentive memory, to determine whether it was an hour or a month ago that a strain was heard among the hundreds played at a sitting, in quick succession.[202]

They were not always successful at eliminating duplicate versions.

By March 1902 the collection was in seven volumes of eighty pages each, averaging twelve music staves of six bars to the page.[203] Two or three playings of a tune were usually sufficient for James O'Neill to capture it in pencil, and most tunes were written at least three times before their final fair copying into manuscript volumes for the engraver.[204] After James had noted a tune to his own satisfaction, Francis listened to his playing of it and, relying on his acute ear and encyclopedic memory, passed final judgement on it. He did not know that James was sometimes playing correctly what he had inadvertently written down incorrectly.[205]

James O'Neill after he became a sergeant

Rather than reproducing exactly what musicians or paper sources provided, as earlier collectors had purported to do and as modern scholarship would demand, O'Neill and his friends took the more robust and pragmatic approach of practising traditional musicians. They invented titles for anonymous tunes, and reset dance music if necessary in keys suitable for fiddle, flute and uilleann pipes. They included only settings they regarded as of merit, and, with a confidence that is hard to criticise, usually preferred their musician sources to printed sources. As James O'Neill said:

Title-page and internal page of one of the O'Neills' manuscripts in 1902

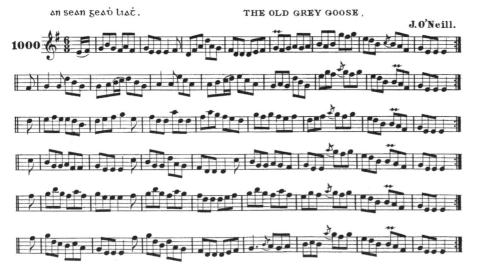

Extreme example of the O'Neills' editing: 'One of the tunes picked up... from John Hicks, the great Irish piper... consisted of the first and third strains... Many years later I heard James Kennedy, a fine fiddler from County Leitrim, play another version of it, being the first and second strains... which he called 'The Geese in the Bog'... Sergt. O'Neill's memory was aroused to the fact that he had a version of this jig among his father's manuscripts. A slight rearrangement resulted in a jig with six strains... To preserve to some extent the connection of the historic and popular fowl with our prize, it was christened "The Old Grey Goose".'

'Not a few of these men have originality in composition... In such cases where we have found a pleasing variation from a set piece we have had no hesitancy in adopting it for it must be Irish'.[206]

Attractive variations from different versions of a tune were sometimes amalgamated without annotation, and bars of music were composed to fill gaps when musicians' memories failed. Without their sources, we have no means of establishing the scale of editing that took place, but it is unlikely to have been very extensive. Francis O'Neill had no apologies for these procedures:

> ... it all depends on individual taste as to which version of a tune is the most meritorious; and as it has been transmitted orally... variants and diversity of settings have naturally multiplied... Why should palpably inferior versions or variants of traditional tunes be exempt from correction or alteration?[207]

The collectors clearly saw themselves as making a collection of tunes for the use of performers, not as making an ethnographic record of performance. Basic melody only was recorded and stylistic features such as variations on repeats,[208] ornamentation and bowing technique almost entirely omitted. O'Neill himself said:

> To illustrate the wealth of graces, turns, and trills, which adorn the performance of capable Irish pipers and fiddlers, skilful both in execution and improvisation, is beyond the scope of exact musical notation.'[209]

Example of a notation giving some stylistic indications

From Francis O'Neill's exasperated comments about the proof reading and corrections involved in the enterprise,[210] it would seem that by this time he had some facility in reading music. It is often said that O'Neill could not read music, but it is certain that he did have a basic literacy in later life.[211]

Although he eventually realised that the sheer variety of Irish music made the project unfeasible, O'Neill had intended to compile a complete encyclopedia of Irish music when he first conceived of publication.[212] Partly this was a symptom of late nineteenth-century New World expansiveness and eagerness to tackle monumental projects, characteristics which fitted in with O'Neill's own ambitious nature. Partly too he was influenced by a tradition of large-scale musical compendia which had been appearing in Britain and America throughout the nineteenth century. One such collection which had been compiled by a fellow Corkman and of which O'Neill was keenly aware was William Forde's *Encyclopaedia of Melody. One Thousand and Twenty-One Airs Selected from the National Music of All Countries,* published in London in the 1840s. In America, and in the area of dance music, Elias Howe of Boston had been publishing large collections of traditional tunes from the 1840s, with titles such as *Howe's One Thousand Jigs and Reels*. One Howe publication which contains a high proportion of Irish tunes and, on the face of it, was an exemplar for O'Neill's first collection is *Ryan's Mammoth Collection. 1050 Reels and Jigs, Hornpipes, Clogs...* of 1883, collected and edited by William Bradbury Ryan, a band-leader in Boston and an assistant of Howe's. This, like O'Neill's, is a classified collection, and it contains many of the Irish dance tunes published by O'Neill, often note for note.[213] While he refers only fleetingly and dismissively to Howe's collections – 'printed in Boston when our parents were young'[214] – and strangely nowhere mentions Ryan's work by title, O'Neill had acquired a copy of it sometime before 1903,[215] and the possibility must remain that he laid it under unacknowledged contribution.[216]

Title-page of Ryan collection

The publication *O'Neill's Music of Ireland*, containing 1850 melodies, 'collected from all available sources',[217] the largest collection of Irish music ever printed, was finally produced by Lyon and Healy of Chicago[218] in the summer of 1903,[219] financed and effectively published by Francis O'Neill in a finely printed and bound edition of 2,000 copies.[220] Over half the contents had been 'noted down from the singing or playing of residents of Chicago',[221] and it was dedicated to O'Neill's own peers, 'the multitude of nonprofessional musicians of the Gaelic and English speaking races all over the world'.[222] The collection was

Title-page and internal page of Francis O'Neill's masterwork

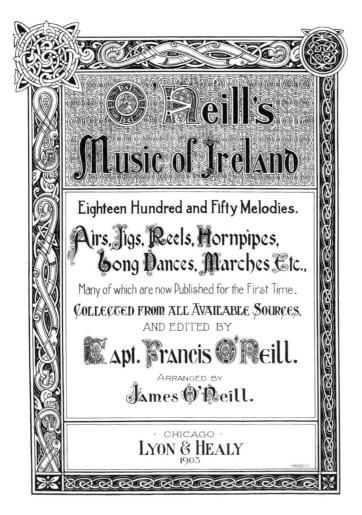

O'Neill's increasing fame brought correspondence to him from all over the world, including in 1902 a music manuscript and a treatise on dance from Patrick D. Reidy in London. Reidy was a Kerry dancing master who taught Gaelic League enthusiasts in London traditional social dances which became the basis in the 1890s of some of the League's ceili dances.

classified by tune-type: song airs (625), Carolan harp tunes (75), double jigs (415), slip jigs (60), reels (380), hornpipes (225), long dances (20), and marches and miscellaneous (50). Alternative titles for tunes were given in the index. Displaying a keen grasp of the value of publicity, Francis gave newspaper interviews about the new work and arranged some thirty reviews in publications appearing from Belfast to Buenos Aires.[223] Although he later discovered that James O'Neill had made errors in key signatures in the work,[224] the publication was received with great acclaim on both sides of the Atlantic, and further afield, from a wide variety of readers. A selection of reactions, which O'Neill printed as testimonials in a later collection, shows the kind of enthusiasm with which it was met:

> A full appreciation of all the treasures contained in the book would take a volume as large as itself.

> To describe adequately this sumptuous quarto volume... would seem flattery...

> No one has ever done anything like this for Irish music.[225]

A musician reader in Australia was even more ecstatic:

> For over a third of a century I have been waiting, watching, hoping and praying, that God might inspire some Irishman, or association of Irishmen, to collect and publish such a work... I thank God that I have lived to see my dreams realised and my prayer answered more fully than my wildest ambitions had dared to go.[226]

Praise however was not unanimous. O'Neill inadvertently walked into sniping fire that Arthur Griffith's pugnacious nationalist periodical *The United Irishman* of Dublin had been anonymously directing at Dr Henebry.[227] The paper was a supporter of the Rev. Edward Gaynor of Cork, also a musical clergyman, who was opposed to Henebry. Henebry, now back in Ireland, had been busy puffing O'Neill's book and basing music theories of his own on tunes taken from it.[228] Anyone he championed had to be cut down, and O'Neill was accused in the paper by an anonymous editorial reviewer in early 1904 of padding his collection with numerous duplicates and variants, and dozens of English airs and ballad tunes.[229] The New York periodical *An Gaodhal (The Gael)* in an unfriendly review quoted choice parts of the Dublin piece and accused O'Neill of trying to get more money for the book from Irish Americans than he was charging in Ireland.[230] O'Neill made a hurt though reasoned reply to the latter review,[231] but the Dublin charges had already been repeated by the Rev. Gaynor in person, writing in *An Claidheamh Soluis*, the newspaper of the Gaelic League,[232] from St Vincent's Church, Cork. He levelled them again a year later.[233] O'Neill eventually saw him off with derision:

> His Reverence, of whose existence we were entirely ignorant, lectured on Irish Music in that famous city, warning his audience against the

Fr Edward Gaynor

great danger to Irish music by the efforts of those who had not the advantage of being born and bred in the real traditional atmosphere, like himself. Why, bless his simple soul! What could have led him to imagine that Watergrass Hill had a monopoly of the traditional atmosphere of County Cork, not to mention the rest of Ireland?[234]

O'Neill was also criticised for including non-traditional Irish tunes such as those of the Dublin-born composer Michael William Balfe:

> The fact that Balfe was a native born Irishman did not save me from the petulant criticisms of some of my best friends for being so deficient in musical discernment. Balfe's music, they contended, was not Irish at all, even if he was.[235]

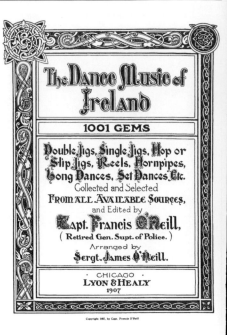

Title-page of 1907 volume

After his retirement from the police force in 1905, O'Neill threw himself with undiminished energy into his musical activities. His next two music publications derived from *O'Neill's Music of Ireland* and were also produced with the assistance of James O'Neill. At the urging of musicians who were interested only in dance music and who needed a cheaper and more focused publication than the deluxe hardback of 1903, O'Neill published in 1907, again through Lyon and Healy in Chicago, *The Dance Music of Ireland*, a classified collection of 1,001 jigs, reels, hornpipes, and special dance tunes. Largely this overlaps in content with the earlier work and shares the same editorial method, but it includes 140 new tunes, according to O'Neill's estimation,[236] and excludes some that had already appeared. This work also was received with acclaim. Being cheaper, it circulated much more widely than the earlier collection, and it is said to have become so pre-eminent in its field that traditional musicians referred to it simply as 'The Book'.[237] In recent decades it has also commonly been called 'The Thousand and One'. Four so-called 'editions' of *The Dance Music of Ireland* were produced by O'Neill,[238] and it has been available in different printings and from different publishers for most of the century. The volume involved O'Neill in an unexpected expense. In spite of James O'Neill's very real musical talents, including his facility at transcription, it seems that he did not have the complete theoretical knowledge required for the enterprise of publication, and that errors made by him and Edward Cronin led to the scrapping of the first two printings of the new work at a cost of $1,200.[239] The plates were saved and corrected as far as practicable and O'Neill privately referred to the volume that actually first appeared as the 'third edition'.[240]

Title-page of 1908 volume

James O'Neill had added a degree of competence in arrangement for the piano to his fiddle skills by the time of Francis O'Neill's next publishing venture, again produced to meet an expressed demand,[241] his *O'Neill's Irish Music. 250 Choice Selections Arranged for Piano and Violin... First Series* of 1908. James provided piano accompaniments for airs and dance tunes drawn from the two earlier publications. The volume may have been partly intended to widen the audience for traditional music to include musicians other than traditional musicians. The latter, who played solo or in unison, were perfectly catered for by the single melody lines of the earlier

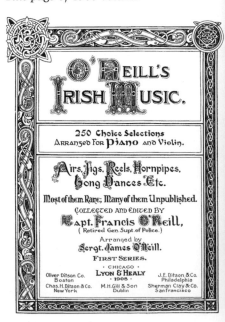

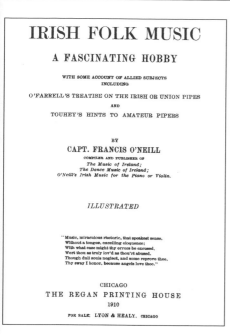

Title-page of 1910 volume, and example of James O'Neill's arrangements for piano

Illustration from the 1910 study: William Rowsome, a piper and pipemaker with whom O'Neill became friendly in Dublin in 1906

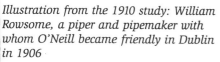

unharmonised works, but other musicians would expect a piano part. James O'Neill's arrangements do not show the influence of formal music study, and were probably evolved while vamping accompaniments by ear. They are not successful as piano pieces, but do have the virtue of generally accommodating the tunes rather than altering them for harmonic purposes. Infelicities however include some inappropriate chromatic notes in the accompaniment for modal tunes, and the settings in general lack flair.[242] Criticisms were expressed of them,[243] and it can be presumed that sales were low as no further series appeared.

Although there is no evidence of a rift between the colleagues, this volume was the last in which James collaborated with Francis. The latter now turned his attention to the production in 1910 of a study of Irish traditional music *Irish Folk Music: A Fascinating Hobby*. This had originated as a contemplated 'series of articles for a publication of wide circulation',[244] and it is an attractive quirky amalgam of autobiography and research, over-formally and over-elaborately expressed for modern taste, but lucid and often trenchant, its narrative well laced with anecdote and humour. It is a work of advocacy, 'full of people'[245] and based on a conviction of the value of Irish traditional music, with a somewhat rose-coloured view of the position of music in the Ireland of his now distant childhood. The opening chapters trace O'Neill's years in Cork and America, largely from a musical perspective, and the later deal with aspects of the general tradition such as the origins and history of tunes, tune titles, early collections, and the fortunes of the music. A particular interest in the history of the uilleann pipes is shown. The non-personal information in the well-indexed volume was drawn from works in his extensive personal library. With the benefit of almost a century of subsequent if patchy research into Irish music, it is easy to criticise the detail of O'Neill's scholarship, which is short on musical analysis, but the book is nevertheless a humane and readable treatment of the subject which shows a clear understanding of the nature of oral tradition. Sympathy can be felt for someone attempting research into a subject at a distance of 4,000 miles.

The Croppies' March

"Patsy" Touhey

75

The teenage Selena O'Neill, and an example of her arrangements for piano

Sometime before 1910 O'Neill made the acquaintance of another namesake, Selena A. O'Neill, a teenage student of the violin at the Chicago Music College[246] whom he and others considered a musical prodigy. Selena was not, as is sometimes said, a relative of Francis's but was the daughter of a fiddle player, another Cork emigrant to Chicago, Tim O'Neill from near Macroom.[247] Her brother John, also a prize-winning violinist, had the better traditional style, O'Neill privately thought,[248] and this verdict seems supported by the commercial recordings of Irish dance music Selena made for the Victor Company in Chicago in 1928 which show her as lacking in traditional fiddle style. She was however almost completely deaf at the time of recording.[249] She had been given piano lessons by the nuns at her parochial school, but her style of piano accompaniment seems to owe more to her association with traditional musicians than to any classical-music training. Her published arrangements, like those of James, do not observe the conventional procedures of harmonic progression, and the resulting texture is often perfuntory and awkward in effect. However, her choice of chords, uninhibited by the conventions of diatonic harmony, allows

Whirlwind dancers? John Ryan, Tipperary; John E. McNamara, Limerick; James P. Coleman, Limerick (left to right): Chicago exhibition stepdancers and dance teachers of O'Neill's acquaintance

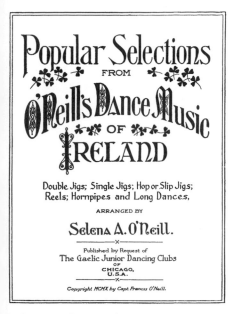

Title-page of 1910 volume

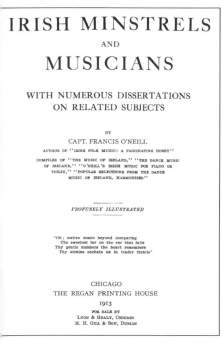

*O'Neill's letter of assignment
to Selena O'Neill*

Title-page of 1913 study

IRISH MINSTRELS
AND
MUSICIANS

WITH NUMEROUS DISSERTATIONS
ON RELATED SUBJECTS

BY

CAPT. FRANCIS O'NEILL

AUTHOR OF "IRISH FOLK MUSIC: A FASCINATING HOBBY"

COMPILER OF "THE MUSIC OF IRELAND," "THE DANCE MUSIC
OF IRELAND," "O'NEILL'S IRISH MUSIC FOR PIANO OR
VIOLIN," "POPULAR SELECTIONS FROM THE DANCE
MUSIC OF IRELAND, HARMONIZED"

PROFUSELY ILLUSTRATED

"Oh; native music beyond comparing
The sweetest far on the ear that falls
Thy gentle numbers the heart remembers
Thy strains enchain us in tender thralls"

CHICAGO
THE REGAN PRINTING HOUSE
1913
FOR SALE BY
LYON & HEALY, CHICAGO
M. H. GILL & SON, DUBLIN

her also to accommodate the character of traditional melodies without altering them chromatically.[250] Recognising this and admiring her musical talent, O'Neill chose her as the arranger of his remaining music collections, and in 1924 assigned control of the 'plates, etchings, electrotypes, halftones, etc. used in the publication of my works' to his 'faithful friend and co-laborer – Selena O'Neill'.[251] In 1940, four years after his death, she used the plates to produce a printing of *The Dance Music of Ireland*.

The first of the works in which Selena O'Neill collaborated was *Popular Selections from O'Neill's Dance Music of Ireland*, published by Francis in 1910 at the 'request of the Gaelic Junior Dancing Clubs of Chicago'.[252] It contains 52 tunes harmonised by Selena, 'one possessed of the ability to give this class of tunes proper musical expression',[253] and was meant for dance classes and competitive step dancing. In a foreword O'Neill warns against dancing too fast and consequently playing music too fast to suit the 'whims of whirlwind dancers'.

Encouraged by the reception given to *Irish Folk Music: A Fascinating Hobby*, O'Neill devoted the next three years to what was originally intended as a revised edition[254] but which grew far beyond its original conception into the monumental *Irish Minstrels and Musicians*. This 500-page book is essentially a biographical compendium, arranged by instrument and chronologically, and compiled from O'Neill's reading and personal experience. Showing again his wide human sympathies and interests, it deals with well over 300 musicians, historical and contemporary. Pipers and pipemakers get the lion's share of the

Far left: One of many historical illustrations in the 1913 volume: Tom Carthy of Ballybunion, Co. Kerry, who lived to the age of 105
Left: A contemporary illustration from the 1913 volume: Fire Captain Michael J. Dunn of Milwaukee, a friend of O'Neill's to whom he gave part of his collection, including cylinders. These were destroyed after Dunn's death.

attention, with fiddle players and harpers coming a poor second and third. Flute players, music collectors and dancing masters figure even less prominently, and players of the accordion, concertina, banjo, mandolin, and mass-produced tin whistle, which were then relatively new instruments in the Irish tradition, hardly rate a mention. The proportions may indicate O'Neill's opinion of the relative importance of each instrument in the tradition, but they also reflect the amounts of historical information available for him to draw upon. There is a concentration on the solo performer, although O'Neill was an enthusiastic group player and often refers to his enjoyment in playing with other musicians. He had a realistic view of the musicians of his acquaintance which is sometimes frankly expressed and sometimes only hinted at. While the volume would benefit from pruning, and the eighteenth- and early nineteenth-century entries could be improved by modern research, and while areas of contemporary Ireland and even of Irish America were only superficially dealt with, O'Neill undertook extensive original and first-hand research into his contemporary musicians (though not singers), exhibiting an enthusiasm and drive that was in no way diminished by his advancing years. He seems to have been motivated not only by a desire to record musicians of the past but also to raise the self-respect of the musicians of his own time.[255] The heavily illustrated resulting volume could not be produced today, and the social picture we have of Irish music would be much poorer without this essential resource which is a starting point for all research into Irish traditional music biography, and a valuable compendium of illustrations. The sheer mass of first-hand evidence it and its 1910 predecessor contain has not yet been assimilated by writers on Irish music. The worth of the new volume was apparent to all but was not reflected in sales:

> Flattering reviews in the press from many quarters, and appreciative comments in other ways, are all that could be desired but orders are disappointingly few.[256]

Selena O'Neill as a graduate

WRITES HISTORY OF IRISH MUSIC

Francis O'Neill, Former Police Chief, Publishes New Volume.

GOES DEEP IN SUBJECT.

Tells Entertainingly Old Erin's Story from Antiquity to Modern Times.

BY JOHN KELLEY.

What is probably the most elaborate history of Irish music ever produced has just been published by Capt. Francis O'Neill, former chief of the Chicago police department. The author has delved deep into the subject—one which is dear to his heart—and, as a result, has brought forth a volume that will be welcomed by the sons and daughters of Erin no matter in what part of the world they reside.

It long has been a cherished ambition of Capt. O'Neill to write such a book for posterity, and after one who is in sympathy with the author's sentiments has perused its pages he can say that he has read the " last word " in Irish music history. It leaves little or nothing to be added on the subject which it treats.

The title of the work is " Irish Minstrels and Musicians." It is dedicated " To the memory of my parents, whose tuneful tastes and memorized melodies are cherished as a most precious heritage."

Not His First Work.

This is not the first book of the kind by

Above: O'Neill went to considerable trouble to publicise, advertise and distribute his works.

Below: Title-page of 1915 volume

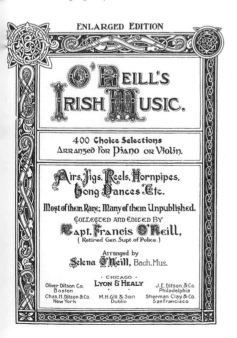

In that same year of 1913 O'Neill was serving on the committee of the recently established Chicago Gaelic Feis,[257] and was a regular attender at the Feis around that time.[258]

By 1915 O'Neill had abandoned his original plan of issuing harmonised versions of Irish tunes in series, and had instead decided on an enlarged edition of his *O'Neill's Irish Music* of 1908, 'a course obviously more economical for all concerned'.[259] This 1915 edition contains 400 tunes arranged by Selena O'Neill – now a Bachelor of Music – for piano or violin. Of the 150 additions at least one-third were appearing in print for the first time,[260] many from manuscripts. Others had been taken from rare out-of-print books. O'Neill, now aged 65, was moving further away from the living tradition and further into the study,[261] and when he says in his foreword that 'In this age of stress and strife, only those possessed of exceptional advantages may hope to gain the publicity so essential to the circulation of a new work, especially one which appeals to a patronage necessarily limited' it seems that his horizons were shrinking. His essential beliefs however were unchanged:

> Irish music... has a beauty, worth, and appeal of its own [which] requires but little harmony...; the peculiar rhythm or swing of Irish dance music... [gives it] its distinctive charm and spirit.[262]

It may be that the latest work met with an inadequate reception. In a letter of 1918 to a clerical friend O'Neill strikes a note of deep disillusion:

> I was music mad, but the fever has subsided considerably. In fact I'm cured. Now I'm only angry, disgusted, and pessimistic. The Irish have frittered away their artistic heritage, and in this generation have come to be regarded by the world at large as nonentities in the arts for which they were most distinguished...[263]

Nevertheless he persevered with his life-work and what he expected to be his 'final contribution to the cherished cause of perpetuating Gaelic musical tradition'.[264] In 1922, when he was 74, he published *Waifs and Strays of Gaelic Melody*, a classified collection of 335 Irish and Scottish melodies harmonised by Selena O'Neill, and – a new departure – with historical and descriptive notes written by himself. The sources for the new collection were chiefly manuscripts that had come to O'Neill from Ireland, England, Australia and various parts of the United States, and rare eighteenth-century collections. Although he speaks of the difficulties of publication being 'most discouraging' in his introduction dated 28 August 1922, a second enlarged edition of the *Waifs and Strays* containing 365 melodies was published. This carries the same dated introduction as the first edition and the same copyright date of 1922, but it cannot also have been published in 1922, given the low expectations of its publisher for the success of the first edition and the fact that the first edition appeared late in the year.[265] The earliest date associated with the second edition is 22 November 1924 which appears on a presentation copy[266], and I feel that this can safely be taken as the year of issue. It is a proper new edition with additional tunes annotated by O'Neill and inserted in their appropriate classified sections, and with a revised index.

Title-page of Waifs and Strays *1st edition (above) and 2nd edition (opposite page)*

In 1931, troubled by deafness and deteriorating eyesight[267] and feeling that he had not long to live, O'Neill made an unconditional gift of his musically rich Irish book library,[268] said to have numbered 1,500 volumes at one stage,[269] and two music manuscripts to the Library of the University of Notre Dame, Indiana, where they still reside. Some musical material, including copies of his books, remained in possession of his family.[270] Other music books and manuscripts, cylinder sound recordings and musical instruments had earlier been presented to musical friends.[271] An amount of this latter material was later destroyed in Milwaukee,[272] but some may still survive. It is remarkable that O'Neill, who was so exercised by the fate of his book collection, did not ensure that his music manuscripts and other papers were permanently secured. It might seem that having gleaned from them all he required he was less anxious about their future, and yet he clearly understood their importance and frequently refers to their value. Selena O'Neill's papers do not survive, having been discarded after her death,[273] and a collection of O'Neill's letters, carefully preserved for decades by relatives in Cork, was said to have been destroyed only weeks before Breandán Breathnach went to seek them out in the 1980s.[274] The recent discovery of two sets of pipes once owned by O'Neill's friend Sergeant Early, to whom O'Neill had presented part of his collection,[275] gives rise to the hope that more items from the collection may yet be found.

Francis O'Neill's interest in Irish music continued until his death. His daughter described him in his later years:

> ... he'd be engrossed in his newspaper, and suddenly something would come to him. Softly, almost surreptitiously, he'd go and

Tune from Hudson manuscript in the O'Neill Collection in Notre Dame Library: one of the few survivors from his manuscript collections

WAIFS and STRAYS
of
GAELIC MELODY

Comprising Forgotten Favorites,
Worthy Variants, and
Tunes not Previously Printed.

Collected and Edited by

Capt. Francis O'Neill

Compiler and Publisher of
"The Music of Ireland," "The Dance Music of Ireland,"
and "O'Neill's Irish Music for Piano or Violin."
AUTHOR OF
"Irish Folk Music—A Fascinating Hobby,"
and "Irish Minstrels and Musicians."

ARRANGED BY

Selena O'Neill, Mus.Bac.

· CHICAGO ·
LYON & HEALY
OLIVER DITSON & CO.   SHERMAN CLAY & CO.   IRISH INDUSTRIAL DEPOT
BOSTON   SAN FRANCISCO   NEW YORK CITY

Copyright MCMXXII. by Capt. Francis O'Neill

play on his whistle until he found the right note. Then he'd write it down.[276]

He wrote occasional articles on Irish music under his own name and ephemeral pseudonyms.[277] Although these hardly contained any unpublished information, they do retain his old vigour and distinctive voice. From its inception in 1930 he was a regular listener to an Irish Hour maintained on Chicago radio by the 'Voice of Labor' and took a keen interest in queries sent to it on the background to tunes and songs.[278] On a visit to the Chicago World Fair in 1934, he sought out a young piper, Joe Shannon, who was playing at the Irish Pavilion, to ask him to play a hornpipe, and presented him with a copy of *Irish Minstrels and Musicians*.[279] Around this time he also briefly met the Cavan and Philadelphia fiddle player and composer Ed Reavy in Chicago.[280] As late as that same year of 1934, at the age of eighty-five, he was still publishing on his old favourite historical topics of Irish dances and dance music.[281] Clearly it was true when he said at the end of his introduction to *Waifs and Strays,* which he intended to be his last published work, that if readers derived as much profit from the work as he had pleasure in compilation and publication then 'all is well, and the desired end has been attained'.

O'Neill's basic motivation in his labours on Irish music was a selfless desire, stemming from his love of the music and the pleasure he found in it, to celebrate, preserve and revive it. National feeling and filial piety were also factors, the wish to collect for posterity the music which he believed was a chief glory of Ireland, and to preserve the west Cork music of his parents and childhood. It was also undoubtedly agreeable to a man of his ambition to receive the international recognition and praise that his work earned him. Financial gain was never a consideration. He freely presented copies of his works to interested people, and arranged with his friend Fr Fielding, when the latter had returned to Ireland, to sell copies of the 1903 book there for less than half its American price in order 'to place before the Irish people their own music'.[282] O'Neill said to a correspondent in 1917 that

Piper Joe Shannon and friends at Chicago World Fair of 1934

IRISH DANCES AND DANCE-MUSIC

THE ORIGIN OF POPULAR TUNES

HISTORY IN MELODY

By CAPTAIN FRANCIS O'NEILL

The author of this article, Captain Francis O'Neill, of Chicago, enjoys international fame as an authority on Irish folk-music. He has made several noted collections of traditional airs. A native of County Cork, the veteran scholar—he is now close on 85 years—has written this interesting and instructive commentary specially for the "Cork Weekly Examiner."

From O'Neill article of 1934 in Cork Weekly Examiner

R. SISK,
The All-Ireland step-dancing champion, member of the Blackpool (Cork) Traditional Step-dancing Club.

> From first to last everything connected with it [the work of collection and publication] was financed by the writer – not to mention the many gratuities inevitable in my intercourse with the class of people from whom cooperation was to be expected. My loss financially ran into the thousands of dollars and even pounds. The exact amount I prefer to forget.[283]

He believed that 'appreciation and patronage'[284] were needed for the survival of Irish music and musicians, and he acted in accordance with his convictions and family traditions in providing them.

The music historian Donal O'Sullivan considered O'Neill to be merely an enthusiast without knowledge,[285] but while O'Neill placed a high value on enthusiasm[286] and could be regarded more as a musical antiquarian than a strict historian, this judgement is inaccurate and ungenerous. O'Neill had an unrivalled knowledge of Irish music from personal experience and study. He often went to great lengths to acquire source material and made a careful reading of his sources, which were often necessarily secondary ones. He resisted unsubstantiated attempts by misguided patriots to ascribe great antiquity to Irish dance music.[287] While he was not ideally located for the academic study of his subject and made a number of mistakes, later historians have followed his outlines and have benefited from reacting against him. Importantly, his artistic and practical achievements in Irish music were all based on a continuous concentration on the music itself. Not least of the virtues of O'Neill's work is its eclecticism:

> … it reflected the various styles and repertories of a wide range of Irish emigré musicians. It suggests that music comes from circumstances, from the actual, from personal encounter… Traditional music, in the real world, does not conform to any one stylistic impulse; if it can be thought of as a musical language, it contains many different dialects, idiolects and accents, and O'Neill's magpie instincts recognised this.[288]

Below: Inscription on 1926 presentation copy of Waifs and Strays *to the motor magnate Henry Ford, who was also of West Cork parentage*

5 LEGACY

Francis O'Neill himself knew that his chief contribution to the work of preserving Irish music lay in the area of dance music, and that in this he had preserved far more than the most active of the earlier collectors. One of his own estimates was that while Edward Bunting had published some 10 dance tunes, George Petrie 170, and Patrick Weston Joyce 140, he himself had published about 1,000 previously unpublished dance tunes, apart altogether from airs, marches, etc.[289] Breandán Breathnach estimated the count as upward of 700.[290] By any reckoning, it was a great harvest. O'Neill was conscious also that he had been enabled to make his contribution by a unique combination of circumstances, both personal and historical:

> The prestige of office and influence, coupled with certain qualities of good fellowship and financial liberality, enabled me to win the confidence and co-operation of people notoriously jealous and secretive. The time was opportune then and will never occur again.[291]

The influence of Francis O'Neill's published collections is difficult to trace in detail, but they have been pervasive in the playing of Irish traditional dance music throughout the twentieth century. Their very existence has been a source of national pride for many in Ireland and in Irish America, not only musicians, and has greatly enhanced the status of traditional dance music in the eyes of its practitioners and their audiences:

> When I was growing up, there was a fiddler in my native village who used to perform a certain ritual before playing a tune. His purpose, of course, was to create a certain air of mystique, and to build up the anticipation of his listeners. He would resin the bow, tune the instrument, and pause before addressing his audience. Then he would announce solemnly: *'This one is from O'Neill's collection'.* Quite obviously, he meant this to be a statement that would put the seal of authenticity on the tune in question.[292]

Set dance or long dance. Almost every example of this sub-genre in existence is in O'Neill's collections.

From the beginning of the century, tunes from the collections have been percolating through the national repertory as literate traditional musicians acquired the volumes of 1903 and especially 1907 on their first appearance, and as a far greater number copied from them into personal manuscripts, sometimes very extensively. These manuscripts were in turn copied, and inherited and used after the death of the original copyists, to such a degree that it is now difficult to establish the content, or the extent, of local repertory before 1903.

Tune copied from O'Neill in an early 20th-century manuscript in Donegal

O'Neill's stamp is nevertheless seen everywhere in the music, even in the nationally known titles of tunes which commemorate his childhood surroundings and his later musical friends and experiences. Ironically, some of the newly discovered tunes which so excited O'Neill and his friends have, through the publications, 'become so well known as to be almost banal'.[293] While his published versions of tunes often replaced those of local oral tradition, the plethora of non-O'Neill versions of O'Neill-published tunes still in circulation provides evidence that their publication did not stultify creativity in the tradition. For some musicians, like Ed Reavy, who was somewhat dissatisfied with O'Neill's versions and unornamented notations, they acted as a spur to creativity.[294]

The publications and the manuscripts boosted the spread of literacy among musicians, and it is certain that O'Neill's collecting and publishing activities were an example for later collectors and publishers such as Francis Roche and Breandán Breathnach. His tune collections also form the basis of Breathnach's Thematic Index of Irish Dance Music which controls over 5,000 tunes.[295] Poets and arrangers also, such as A.P. Graves and Sir Charles Stanford,[296] mined his collections for suitable melodies.

Among non-literate traditional musicians the influence of the publications was no less. They learned O'Neill's music by ear from the playing of their literate fellow musicians. The example of concertina player Paddy Murphy and other musicians of the Connolly-Kilmaley area of west Clare taught in the 1930s by Hughdie Doohan, the local postman and a literate fiddle player who owned a copy of *The Dance Music of Ireland,* would have been typical of many:

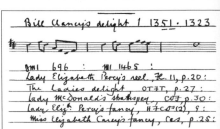

Breandán Breathnach and one of his manuscript index cards. The notations DMI (O'Neill's 1907 collection) and MI (1903 collection) are frequently the first entries on a Breathnach card.

Hughdie used to sit down like any good schoolmaster with the lamp in front of him on the table. The book would be taken down and Hughdie's fiddle tuned to perfection. He would read the music then from O'Neill's book and according as Hughdie read them we learned them off. He was a mighty man for strange and new tunes. It was from Hughdie that we got Kit O'Mahony's Jig, The Flax in Bloom, The Maid of Feakle, The Northern Lassies and loads more. None of them tunes were ever heard of around here until Hughdie started to read them off of the book.[297]

Paddy Murphy (top centre) and friends in Clare in the 1940s. 'The Maid of Feakle' was collected by O'Neill in east Clare in 1906 and may have been named by him for Anna O'Neill who was a native of Feakle.

Non-literate players learned especially from musicians on commercial sound recordings who, from the 1920s, were drawing on his collections and crediting him as a source in studio log-books. Perhaps even more of the tunes preserved by O'Neill were put into circulation by Irish radio from 1926, as regular radio performers tended to be literate and had a continuous need for a supply of unhackneyed melodies. The ceili bands, which were in their heyday from the 1930s to the early 1960s, also frequently drew repertory from O'Neill's collections. The revival of interest in traditional music which began to gather pace in the 1950s and which has continued to the present day led to a demand for O'Neill's works which brought about their frequent reprinting. The sleeve-notes of modern LPs and CDs frequently credit the O'Neill collections as sources, and they are regarded as the standard collections of non-contemporary Irish traditional music.

Sligo virtuoso fiddle player Michael Coleman's recordings of the O'Neills' 'The Old Grey Goose', which he called 'The Grey Goose', have made it a standard item of the national repertory.

HAYES, Middlesex.

WALSH. Mr.Liam.   IRISH PIPE SOLOS.

No.		TITLE	DATE		COMPOSER	PUBLISHER	COPYRIGHTED BY
		E.JACKSON & A.D.LAWRENCE IN "A" STUDIO. HAYES.		Sept:		(From O'Neill's)	
6660	1	Drimmen Dhoun Dheelich.(The faithful Brownoow.).	22-5-25	8-25	Traditional.	"Music of Ireland")	
6660	2	" "	5-6-24	"	"	(Published by)	
						(Lyon & Healy.1903.)	
6661	1	Billy Taylor's Fancy.	26-6-25	"	"	"	
6661	2	"	1-11-23	"	"	"	
6662	1	The Mountain Lark. "Dan McCarthy's Fancy."	26-6-25	"	"	"	
6662	2	" "	22-4-25	"	"	"	
6663	1	The Cliffs of Moher. Saddle the pony.	16-7-24	"	"	"	
6663	2	" "		"	"	"	

In the light of all this, it does not seem an exaggeration to say that O'Neill's was the greatest individual influence on the evolution of Irish traditional dance music in the twentieth century. A forthcoming massive single-volume edition of his music containing more than 2,500 tunes, of which this present work is a forerunner and companion volume, appearing as it will close to the end of the century, will copperfasten that influence.[298]

It is a pity that all O'Neill's selfless efforts to preserve and promote Irish music and Irish musicians did not meet with a greater response in his own lifetime, and that he did not live to see the later revitalisation of the music to which he himself would contribute from the grave. But his colourful story and his contribution to Irish culture have never been entirely forgotten down the years, although they have sometimes been ignored. In death, as in life, he has been good copy. Irregular coverage of his career and achievements in popular newspapers, magazines and radio programmes has fostered a general aware-

Above left: Waterford piper Liam Walsh and his acknowledgements to O'Neill in a HMV studio log-book of 1925

Above right: Galway accordion player Máirtín O'Connor and his acknowledgements to O'Neill on a 1990s CD reissued from a 1970s LP

Micheál Ó Riabhaigh (fourth piper from left) and members of the Cork Pipers' Club in Tralibane in 1964

ness of his importance among people interested in traditional music. As can be seen in the Appendix below, a remarkable number of reprints of the original O'Neill volumes have been produced since the mid-1960s, many of them works of *pietas* rather than commercial ventures, and tens of thousands of copies have been sold.[299] Micheál Ó Riabhaigh, who revived the Cork Pipers' Club in the early 1960s, led an annual excursion of pipers to play in O'Neill's memory at Tralibane Bridge before his death in 1976,[300] and compiled and presented a series of radio programmes on O'Neill in 1969. *Treoir,* the house magazine of Comhaltas Ceoltóirí Éireann, has reprinted occasional brief extracts from O'Neill's works since 1969. Original research on O'Neill was undertaken and published by Barry O'Neill and Breandán Breathnach in the 1970s.[301] In 1976 American fiddle player Miles Krassen produced a new edition of the dance and harp tunes in O'Neill's 1903 volume, making 'corrections' and substituting more modern settings for those of O'Neill.[302] In 1978 the Cork Pipers' Club and Comhaltas Ceoltóirí Éireann, the Cork City branch of which had been named after O'Neill, organised open-air music sessions in his honour at the crossroads in Tralibane which saw a crowd of over 1,000 people coming from all over the country.[303] RTÉ radio producer Proinsias Ó Conluain researched and broadcast on O'Neill in the 1970s. Ethnomusicologist Paulette Gershen completed a thesis on O'Neill in the Folklore Department, University of California at Los Angeles, in 1989. RTÉ radio producer Harry Bradshaw has lectured extensively on O'Neill in Ireland and America in recent years. A site for a memorial monument to Francis O'Neill has recently been acquired by local effort in Tralibane close to his birthplace.

O'Neill is also appropriately remembered among Irish musicians in Chicago, where commemorative activities range from annual personal visits to his grave to the teaching of traditional music in classes. A Francis O'Neill Music Club was founded in the city in 1977.[304] Researchers in Chicago such as Jim McGuire, Kevin Henry,

Gathering of musicians in O'Neill's memory, Tralibane, c. 1970

Noel Rice and Bill Currie have also undertaken personal research into O'Neill, and some have published and lectured on him. The major libraries of his adopted city however have none or few of his published works. Over 90 miles away, in Notre Dame University, South Bend, Indiana, his book collection, which had been enthusiastically received by the university authorities in 1931[305] but which had been dispersed for years among the university's general holdings, was reassembled as a single collection at the end of the 1980s.[306] Properly housed and preserved, it is recognised by the University as an important accession of its library's Department of Special Collections, and was the subject of a special exhibition there in 1990.[307]

Although he settled in America during the long period of Irish Famine emigration there, Francis O'Neill was really a type of the pre-Famine emigrant: a younger son of a relatively well-off family who left Ireland for adventure and advancement. He found both, probably to a degree beyond his expectations when he was chafing against the monotony of country life in Tralibane. In those days however he could hardly have conceived that he would be remembered indefinitely for his work in the preservation and dissemination of the traditional music which was all around him and which would occupy him throughout his life, but it is certain that he will. Because of his remarkably conscious and analytical memory for music, his collections will grow rather than decline in importance as Irish traditional instrumental music prepares to enter the next century and next millennium in a vigorous condition; the increasingly electronic transmission and mediation of the music will only alter their formats and increase their influence. O'Neill's publications are the largest snapshot of this music ever taken in its 9,000-year history. They will always retain their unique position in the documentation of recent centuries, and will remain an essential reference-point for future researchers. For musicians they will remain what they were intended to be: an essential induction into the Irish tradition and a treasure trove of music of the past for future use.

MUSIC MAD

Captain Francis O'Neill

and

Traditional Irish Music

An Exhibition from the Captain
Francis O'Neill Collection of Irish Music
March, 1990--August, 1990

Compiled by Laura Sue Fuderer

Department of Special Collections
University Libraries
University of Notre Dame
Notre Dame, Indiana
1990

Title-page of Notre Dame exhibition catalogue

Bookplate on volume from the O'Neill collection in Notre Dame Library

Library of
Capt. Francis O'Neill
Chicago

CAPT. FRANCIS O'NEILL.

seilʒ an maoraoin ruaó.   THE FOX CHASE.

Tuohy.

The final item in O'Neill's 1903 volume: one of the few pieces of programme music in the Irish tradition. Supposedly composed originally on a traditional song air by a Tipperary piper Edmund Keating Hyland about 1800, this version preserved by O'Neill he attributed to Patsy Touhey who had received it from John Smithwick Wayland in Cork who had primarily learned it from Mrs Bridget Kenny in Dublin (but see Donnelly 1993).

APPENDIX

BOOKS BY FRANCIS O'NEILL

1903 **O'Neill's / Music of Ireland / Eighteen Hundred and Fifty Melodies. / Airs, Jigs, Reels, Hornpipes, / Long Dances, Marches Etc., / Many of which are now Published for the First Time. / Collected from all Available Sources, / and edited by / Capt. Francis O'Neill. / Arranged by James O'Neill. / Chicago / Lyon & Healy / 1903**

Reverse of title-page: Copyright 1903 / by / FRANCIS O'NEILL.

31 cm. Hardback, gilt, $5.00. Pp. [xiii] + 366 (= 1: illustration + 9: introductory + 3: illustrations + 349: music + 1: classification + 16: classified index).[308]

Facsimile reprints:[309]
- *O'Neill's Music of Ireland. Eighteen Hundred and Fifty Melodies...*, Daniel Michael Collins, New York 1963. (paperback, early issues with plastic comb spine; reprinted c. 1972, etc., until reissued as Rockchapel edition below)
- *The Great Irish Song Book. More than 1000 Songs and Dances of the Irish People...*, Hansen House, Miami Beach 1976. (paperback; partial reprint with approx. 1000 tunes reordered and renumbered, and with guitar chords added)
- *O'Neill's Music of Ireland. Eighteen Hundred and Fifty Melodies...*, Rockchapel Press, Ho-ho-kus, New Jersey 1979. (paperback; reissued as Mel Bay edition below)
- *O'Neill's Music of Ireland. Eighteen Hundred and Fifty Melodies...*, Mel Bay Publications, Pacific, Missouri n.d. [1996] (paperback)

New edition:
- Miles Krassen ed., *O'Neill's Music of Ireland. New and revised*, Oak Publications, New York 1976 (paperback; omits airs and some 180 dance tunes)

1907 **The Dance Music of / Ireland / 1001 gems / Double Jigs, Single Jigs, Hop or / Slip Jigs, Reels, Hornpipes, / Long Dances, Set Dances Etc. / Collected and Selected / From all Available Sources, / and Edited by / Capt. Francis O'Neill, / (Retired Gen. Supt. of Police.) / Arranged by / Sergt. James O'Neill. / Chicago / Lyon & Healy / 1907 / Copyright 1907, by Capt. Francis O'Neill**

31 cm. Hardback, $ 2.00 later $2.75; paperback, $1.50 later $2.00. Pp. 174 (= 5: introductory + 8: classified index + 3: illustrations + 156: music + 1: classification + 1: advertisements on cover).

Facsimile reprints:
- *The Dance Music of Ireland. 1001 Gems...*,[310] Lyon & Healy, Chicago 1907 [but post-1907?] (hardback with photos of Irish-based musicians)
- *The Dance Music of Ireland. 1001 Gems...* '3rd edition', Lyon & Healy, Chicago 1907 [but post-1907] (paperback)
- *The Dance Music of Ireland. 1001 Gems...* '4th edition', Lyon & Healy, Chicago 1907 [but post-1907] (paperback)

- *The Dance Music of Ireland. 1001 Gems...*, Selena O'Neill, Chicago 1940 (paperback)
- *The Dance Music of Ireland. Book One. 157 Double Jigs, Single Jigs, Hop or Slip Jigs, Reels, Hornpipes, Long Dances, Set Dances, etc...*, Irish Music Corporation of America, Chicago 1959 (paperback; reprint of part of each of the classified sections)
- *The Dance Music of Ireland. Book Two. 171 Tunes...*, Irish Music Corporation of America, Chicago 1962 (paperback; reprint of part of each of the classified sections. Other books in this series were intended, but none were published.)
- *The Dance Music of Ireland. 1001 Gems...*, Walton's Musical Instrument Galleries, Dublin n.d. [1965] (hardback and paperback; black on green cover with harp illustration; cover title: '1001 Gems. The Dance Music of Ireland. O'Neill')
- *The Dance Music of Ireland. 1001 Gems...*, Walton's Musical Instrument Galleries, Dublin n.d. [copyright 1965 but 1970s] (paperback; ; multi-coloured lettering on white cover; cover title: 'O'Neill's 1001 Jigs, Reels, Hornpipes, Airs & Marches. The Irish Music Collection...')
- *The Dance Music of Ireland. 1001 Gems...*, Walton's Musical Instrument Galleries, Dublin 1986 (paperback; photographic cover; cover title: 'O'Neill's 1001 Jigs, Reels, Hornpipes, Airs and Marches. The Irish Music Collection')
- *The Lords of the Dance. Book One...*, Pat Roche, Chicago 1990 (paperback; includes a reprint of 6 pages)

1908 **O'Neill's / Irish Music. / 250 Choice Selections / Arranged for Piano and Violin. / Airs, Jigs, Reels, Hornpipes, / Long Dances Etc. / Most of them Rare; Many of them Unpublished. / Collected and Edited By / Capt. Francis O'Neill, / (Retired Gen. Supt. of Police.) / Arranged by / Sergt. James O'Neill. / First Series / Chicago / Lyon & Healy / 1908 / Oliver Ditson Co. / Boston / Chas. H. Ditson & Co. / New York / M.H. Gill & Son / Dublin / J.E. Ditson & Co. / Philadelphia / Sherman Clay & Co. / San Francisco**

31 cm. Hardback $2.00, paperback $1.50. Pp. 125 (= 1: advertisement + 2: introductory + 3: classified index + 1: illustration + 117: music + 1: advertisement).

1910 **IRISH FOLK MUSIC / A FASCINATING HOBBY / with some account of allied subjects / including / O'FARRELL'S TREATISE ON THE IRISH OR UNION PIPES / and / TOUHEY'S HINTS TO AMATEUR PIPERS / BY / CAPT. FRANCIS O'NEILL / compiler and publisher of / The Music of Ireland; / The Dance Music of Ireland; / O'Neill's Irish Music for the Piano or Violin. / ILLUSTRATED / "Music, miraculous rhetoric, that speakest sense... " / CHICAGO / THE REGAN PRINTING HOUSE / 1910 / FOR SALE: LYON & HEALY, Chicago**

Reverse of title-page: Copyright 1910. / by / CAPT. FRANCIS O'NEILL

24 cm. Hardback, $2.00. Pp. 359 including index and three appendices: A on O'Farrell's instructions for the uilleann pipes; B 'Hints to Amateur Pipers, by Patrick J. Touhey, the Celebrated Performer on the Irish Pipes'; C a supplement of 13 tunes illustrating change in Irish music.

24 plates.

Facsimile reprints:
- *Irish Folk Music: A Fascinating Hobby*, Norwood Editions, Darby, Pennsylvannia 1973. With a new introduction by Barry O'Neill (hardback)
- *Irish Folk Music: A Fascinating Hobby*, EP Publishing, Wakefield 1973. With a new introduction by Barry O'Neill (hardback; reprinted 1977)
- *Irish Folk Music: A Fascinating Hobby*, Folcroft Library Editions, Folcroft, Pennsylvannia 1975. With a new introduction by Barry O'Neill (hardback)

- *Irish Folk Music: A Fascinating Hobby,* R. West, Philadelphia 1977. With a new introduction by Barry O'Neill (hardback)

1910 **Popular Selections / from / O'Neill's Dance Music / of / Ireland / Double Jigs; Single Jigs; Hop or Slip Jigs; Reels; Hornpipes and Long Dances, / arranged by / Selena A. O'Neill. / Published by Request of / The Gaelic Junior Dancing Clubs / of / Chicago, / U.S.A. / Copyright MCMX by Capt. Francis O'Neill**

30 cm. Paperback, 60c. Pp. 26 (= 2: introductory + 1: classified index + 21: music + 2: advertisements on covers).

Facsimile reprint:
- *Popular Selections from O'Neill's Dance Music of Ireland...,* Walton's Musical Instrument Galleries, Dublin 1965 (paperback)

1913 **IRISH MINSTRELS / AND / MUSICIANS / WITH NUMEROUS DISSERTATIONS / ON RELATED SUBJECTS / BY / CAPT. FRANCIS O'NEILL / AUTHOR OF "IRISH FOLK MUSIC: A FASCINAT-ING HOBBY" / COMPILER OF "THE MUSIC OF IRELAND", "THE DANCE MUSIC / OF IRELAND", "O'NEILL'S IRISH MUSIC FOR PIANO OR / VIOLIN", "POPULAR SELECTIONS FROM THE DANCE / MUSIC OF IRELAND, HARMONISED" / PROFUSELY ILLUSTRATED / "Oh; native music beyond comparing... " / CHICAGO / THE REGAN PRINTING HOUSE / 1913 / FOR SALE BY / Lyon & Healy, Chicago / M.H. Gill & Son, Dublin**

Reverse of title-page: Copyright 1913 / by / CAPT. FRANCIS O'NEILL

25 cm. Hardback, gilt, $2.50 later $3.00. Pp. 497 including 99 illustrations, music examples and index.

55 plates.

Facsimile reprints:
- *Irish Minstrels and Musicians, with Numerous Dissertations on Related Subjects,* Norwood Editions, Darby, Pennsylvannia 1973. With a new introduction by Barry O'Neill (hardback)
- *Irish Minstrels and Musicians, with Numerous Dissertations on Related Subjects,* EP Publishing, Wakefield 1973. With a new introduction by Barry O'Neill (hardback)
- *Irish Minstrels and Musicians, with Numerous Dissertations on Related Subjects,* Folcroft Library Editions, Folcroft, Pennsylvannia 1975. With a new introduction by Barry O'Neill (hardback)
- *Irish Minstrels and Musicians, with Numerous Dissertations on Related Subjects,* R. West, Philadelphia 1977. With a new introduction by Barry O'Neill (hardback)
- *Irish Minstrels and Musicians, with Numerous Dissertations on Related Subjects,* Arden Library, New York 1983. With a new introduction by Barry O'Neill (hardback)
- *Irish Minstrels And Musicians, with Numerous Dissertations on Related Subjects,* Mercier Press, Cork & Dublin 1987. With introductory article 'Francis O'Neill, Collector of Irish Music' by Breandán Breathnach, reprinted from *Dal gCais* no 3 (1977) [(paperback; cover title: 'Irish Minstrels and Musicians. The Story of Irish Music']
- *Irish Minstrels And Musicians, with Numerous Dissertations on Related Subjects,* Celtic Music, Louth, Lincolnshire 1987 (paperback)

1915 **O'Neill's / Irish Music. / 400 Choice Selections / Arranged for Piano or Violin. / Airs, Jigs, Reels, Hornpipes, / Long Dances Etc. / Most of them Rare; Many of them Unpublished. / Collected and Edited By / Capt. Francis O'Neill, / (Retired Gen. Supt. of Police.) / Arranged by / Selena O'Neill, Bach. Mus. / Chicago / Lyon & Healy / Oliver Ditson Co. / Boston / Chas. H. Ditson & Co. / New York / M.H. Gill & Son / Dublin / J.E. Ditson & Co. / Philadelphia / Sherman Clay & Co. / San Francisco/ ENLARGED EDITION***

* This edition note is at top of page.

N.D. [1915]

30 cm. Edition de luxe (six copies only); Hardback, $2.75; paperback, $2.00. Pp. ix + 181 (= 1: advertisement + 3: introductory + 4: classified index and classification + 1: illustration + 181: music).

Facsimile reprint:
- *O'Neill's Irish Music. 400 Choice Selections… Enlarged Edition,* The Mercier Press, Cork & Dublin 1987 (paperback)

1922 **Waifs and Strays / of / Gaelic Melody / Comprising Forgotten Favorites, / Worthy Variants, and / Tunes not Previously Printed. / Collected and Edited by / Capt. Francis O'Neill / Compiler and Publisher of / "The Music of Ireland", "The Dance Music of Ireland", / and "O'Neill's Irish Music for Piano or Violin". / author of / "Irish Folk Music – A Fascinating Hobby", / and "Irish Minstrels and Musicians". / Arranged by / Selena O'Neill, Mus. Bac. / Chicago / Lyon & Healy / Oliver Ditson & Co. / Boston / Sherman Clay & Co. / San Francisco / Irish Industrial Depot / New York City / Copyright MCMXXII, by Capt. Francis O'Neill**

31 cm. Hardback, price unknown. Pp. 172 (= 7: introductory + 3: classified index + 2: illustrations + 160: music).

1924 **Waifs and Strays / of / Gaelic Melody / Comprising Forgotten Favorites, / Worthy Variants, and / Tunes not Previously Printed. / Collected and Edited by / Capt. Francis O'Neill / Compiler and Publisher of / "The Music of Ireland", "The Dance Music of Ireland", / and "O'Neill's Irish Music for Piano or Violin". / author of / "Irish Folk Music – A Fascinating Hobby", / and "Irish Minstrels and Musicians". / Arranged by / Selena O'Neill, Mus. Bac. / Chicago / Lyon & Healy / Oliver Ditson & Co. / Boston / Sherman Clay & Co. / San Francisco / Irish Industrial Depot / New York City / Copyright MCMXXII, by Capt. Francis O'Neill / SECOND EDITION – Enlarged***

* This edition note is at top of page.

Believed actually published 1924

31 cm. Hardback, $2.75; paperback, $2.00. Pp. 187 (= 1: advertisement + 4.5: introductory + 2.5: classified index + 1: illustration + 178: music).

Facsimile reprint:
- *Waifs and Strays of Gaelic Melody… Second Edition – Enlarged,* The Mercier Press, Cork & Dublin 1980 (paperback)

NOTES

My main aim in this publication has been to summarise the known facts about Francis O'Neill and indicate the scope of his work in Irish music. I have relied chiefly on O'Neill's own writings, on Irish primary sources, and on early published Chicago sources, for some of which O'Neill supplied information. In order to reduce the number of footnotes, chapters 1-3 of O'Neill's *Irish Folk Music: A Fascinating Hobby* (1910), in which he concentrates on his own life and involvement with music, have been taken as a base text. Unattributed biographical facts are from these chapters. Copies of letters and typescripts cited without a location reference are in the Irish Traditional Music Archive, Dublin. The spelling and punctuation of sources have been retained in quotations. For explanation of abbreviated references see Information Sources below.

1. Ffrench 1897: 308. Griffith 1853: passim shows Daniel Mahony as a holder of extensive land and houses in the parish of Drimoleague and neighbourhood. His dates and those of his wife are calculated from the inscription on a memorial gravestone O'Neill erected to his maternal grandparents in Castletownkinneigh cemetery, Co. Cork, in 1906. I am obliged to Harry Bradshaw for direction to the gravestone. A hornpipe in O'Neill 1903: 294 is named 'Big Dan O'Mahony'. The Kean Mahonys or Mahony Keans – Ó Mathúna Cianach in Irish – are a branch of the O'Mahonys which may be named after Cian, father of the 11th-century Mahon who was a grandson of Brian Boru and gave his name to the sept (Ó Mathghamhna 1974: 3-4). O'Neill partly re-Gaelicised the names of his relatives who, on official documents such as baptismal registers and property valuations, are shown as using anglicised forms of their names.
2. O'Neill 1910a: 117.
3. These dates and those of his father below are calculated from the inscription on a memorial gravestone O'Neill erected to his parents in old Caheragh cemetery, Co. Cork, in 1906. Again I am obliged to Harry Bradshaw for direction to the gravestone.
4. Ffrench 1897: 308. Griffith 1853: 11, 35 shows John Neill holding a house, offices and 25 acres of middling land in Tralibane, 35 acres in Colomane West, and other land and houses in neighbouring townlands, sometimes in partnership with a Philip Neill who held 33 good acres in Tralibane. This was presumably his brother and the same Philip Neill who acted as the baptismal sponsor of Francis (see Note 9). Other Neills held land in neighbouring townlands. The O'Neill house in Tralibane was locally regarded as a fine building (Mrs Catherine Mulhall, Tralibane, pers. comm., July 1996).
5. Tralibane, also spelt Trawlebane and otherwise, is a townland of 497 acres. Its name in Irish *Trá*

a' Leadhbáin (The strand of the little strip of land) is a reference to a strand which fringed the River Owenashingane. The parish of Caheragh, in which Tralibane is, was exceptionally dedicated to religion and learning. Twenty-one Massrocks were located there in penal times. In 1824 there were said to be five hedge-schools in the parish, and a slated schoolhouse was built there in 1827 (O'Donoghue n.d.: 53).
6. O'Neill 1910a: 76.
7. O'Neill 1910a: 72, 143.
8. O'Neill 1910a: 116.
9. O'Neill's entry in a baptismal register of Caheragh Catholic Church shows him being baptised 'Dan. of John Neil & Cathr Mahoney' on 30 August 1848, the sponsors being Philip Neil and Ellen Donovan. I am obliged for access to the register to Fr Michael O'Donovan, P.P., Caheragh. That he was officially 'Daniel Francis' is confirmed by an inscription he himself had placed in 1906 on the memorial to his maternal grandfather in Castletownkinneigh, Co. Cork, and by O'Brien 1904: 226.
10. His death certificate, for which information was supplied by his daughter Mary. The year of birth is confirmed by the baptismal register, by Flinn 1887: 463, and by some of his obituaries. Ffrench 1897: 310 gives 25 August 1849 as the date of birth and this has been commonly followed, but no one of the name was baptised in Tralibane in August 1849 according to the baptismal register (Fr Michael O'Donovan, pers. comm., March 1995).
11. The six older siblings were Philip (baptised 17 Jan. 1835), Mary (bap. 6 July 1836, seemingly known as Nancy), John (bap. 17 July 1838), Michael (bap. 15 Jan. 1841, seemingly died young), Catherine (bap. 19 Sept. 1843), and another Michael (bap. 1 Oct. 1845). Again I am obliged to Fr Michael O'Donovan for this information from the baptismal register. In 1912 O'Neill mentions sending books to his 'brother

and sister in West Carbery' (letter from O'Neill to Séamus Ó Casaide, 15 May 1912 (National Library of Ireland MS 8116 (6)). Nancy had settled in Chicago before 1910 (O'Neill 1910: 116).

12. For the Famine in O'Neill's native area see Hickey 1995: 185-203.
13. Hourihan 1977: 92-6.
14. Harrison 1992: 33.
15. It is interesting that another important traditional music collector, the Rev. James Goodman (1828-96), a clergyman of the Church of Ireland from Kerry who later became professor of Irish in Trinity College Dublin, was a curate at Ardgroom, Co. Cork, some forty miles from Tralibane, in the 1860s. He was fair-copying his collection there from 1861, while O'Neill was still at national school. A flute player from his youth, like O'Neill, Goodman is said to have learned to play the uilleann pipes in Ardgroom. While O'Neill did not know Goodman personally, he includes an admiring biography of him in his *Irish Minstrels and Musicians* of 1913, and clearly identified with him to a degree. The Goodman collection has been edited for publication by Hugh Shields.
16. The Irish terms mean 'Cormac of the prayers' and 'The fair-haired piper' respectively.
17. O'Neill 1910a: 13-14. Hagerty also made an impression on Patrick 'Rocky Mountain' O'Brien, an early schoolmate of O'Neill's who later became a well known Fenian in the United States and author of O'Brien 1904. O'Brien commemorated Hagerty in verse, as illustrated.
18. O'Brien 1904: 106. I am obliged to Fr Michael O'Donovan for bringing this source to my attention and for making it available to me.
19. Harrison 1992: 23.
20. O'Neill 1910a: 12, and O'Neill 1903: Notice before Introduction.
21. Dates calculated from memorial gravestone in old Caheragh cemetery, Co. Cork. Griffith 1853: 11 shows Timothy Downing holding houses and 120 acres of land in Tralibane.
22. See Note 211 below.
23. According to the national census of 1851, 29% of the population of the barony of Bantry were monoglot Irish speakers and 50-60% could speak both Irish and English (Nic Craith 1993: 69-88). O'Neill says that Irish was 'much spoken' in Tralibane in the years after the Famine, and that local children who were not educated in English received oral religious instruction in Irish (O'Neill 1910a: 13).
24. O'Neill 1903: Notice before Introduction. O'Neill thanks an author friend Fr John J. Carroll, who was prominent in Chicago Gaelic League circles and preached in Irish in the city, for 'arranging and perfecting the bilingual names of the Melodies' (O'Neill 1903: 5 of Introduction). He himself may have made the initial draft translations. Whoever did, the results are reasonably idiomatic but not error-free. No accents are used, and typographical and grammatical mistakes appear.

25. Craoibhín 1937: 58. The meeting took place in Bernard Delaney's residence on Forest Avenue (O'Neill 1910a: 222) and the unmusical Hyde recorded the occasion in his diary entry for 12 Jan. 1906 :

Do chaith mé an tráthnóna le Mac Uí Néill, uachtarán na bPóilíní, tráth, agus atá ar phinnsiún anois. Badh é an tAthair Ó Fithcheallaigh do thug amach mé... Anocht bhí lucht rinnce, lucht abhráin, lucht píobaireachta, agus ceoltóirí eile, cruinnighthe aige [Ó Néill], agus do lean an sluagh do'n rinnce agus do'n cheol ar feadh dhá uair a' chluig nó trí. Ba Ghaedhilgeóirí an chuid ba mhó aca, agus bhí na rinnceóirí ar fheabhas. Do bhronn sé leabhar mór fonn orm do bhí clóbhuailte aige. Tháinig mé abhaile ar leath-uair tar éis a haon-déag. (Craoibhín, op. cit., loc. cit.)

I spent the evening with O'Neill, the former chief of police who is now on pension. It was Father Fielding who brought me out... Tonight he [O'Neill] had gathered dancers, singers, pipers, and other musicians, and they all kept up the dancing and the music for two or three hours. Most of them were Irish speakers, and the dancers were excellent. He presented me with a large book of tunes which he has had printed. I came home at half-past eleven. (present writer's translation)

26. O'Neill 1910a: 223.
27. Letter from O'Neill to Séamus Ó Casaide, 23 Mar. 1911 (National Library of Ireland MS 8116 (5)).
28. A typescript listing of his library in 1919 is in the Department of Special Collections in the Hesburgh Library of the University of Notre Dame.
29. O'Neill 1924, see Note 266 below.
30. O'Brien 1904: 248.
31. This was not the same school which O'Neill's contemporary Tim Healy, later Parnell's lieutenant and the first governor-general of the Irish Free State, attended in the early 1860s in Bantry, as described by Liam O'Flaherty in O'Flaherty 1927: 22, 31 (Mrs Kathleen O'Riordan, Bantry Historical Society, pers. comm., Aug. 1996).
32. Anon. 1901: 38.
33. Ffrench 1897: 311.
34. 'When barely sixteen and with the limited capital of five dollars he left home...' (Anon. 1905: 278).
35. Ffrench 1897: 311.
36. Letter from O'Neill to Rev. Seamus Ó Floinn, 15 Oct. 1918 (Dept of Special Collections, Hesburgh Library, Notre Dame University, Indiana).
37. Some sources (Anon. 1901: 38, for instance) state that O'Neill lost his way to the bishop's house and failed to turn up for an appointment. The bishop had left Cork by the following day, and O'Neill had missed his first vocation.
38. Anon. 1936a: 7.
39. Captain's manifest for the Emerald Isle, comm-

unicated by Harry Bradshaw.
40. O'Neill 1910a: 121-2.
41. *Chicago Daily Tribune,* 30 Apr. 1901: 3.
42. Ibid.
43. Anon. 1936a: 7.
44. Griffin 1990: 38.
45. Letter from O'Neill to A.P. Graves, 20 Nov. 1906.
46. French 1897: 312.
47. Ibid.: 314. The place of marriage is given as Normal, Illinois, in the *Irish Independent* version of O'Neill's obituary (see Anon. 1936a).
48. Ó Riabhaigh 1969b: Programme 3, and O'Neill 1910a: 79. Ó Riabhaigh was friendly in Cork with O'Neill's nephew Fr John O'Neill, who was professor of Classics in St Patrick's College, Maynooth, from 1928 to 1941. He had stayed with the O'Neills in Chicago when studying for the degree of M. Phil. at university there.
49. Anon. 1905: 279.
50. This paragraph in general summarises Ffrench 1897: 311-3 who states that O'Neill joined the force on 12 July. O'Neill's obituary (Anon. 1936a) gives the date as 15 July, Flinn 1887: 463 as 17 July.
51. McCaffrey 1987: 3.
52. Funchion 1976: 42.
53. McCaffrey 1987: 7.
54. Figures in this paragraph are based on those quoted in Griffin 1990: 111; Blessing 1980: 531; and McCullough 1978: 26-7.
55. Rehm 1874: passim.
56. O'Neill 1913: 376-7.
57. Anon. 1905: 279.
58. Ibid. A wound he sustained in the left hand still gave him twinges more than twenty-five years later (*Chicago Sunday Tribune,* 2 Feb. 1902: 48).
59. Anon. 1901: 38.
60. *Chicago Sunday Tribune,* 25 Aug. 1901: 38.
61. *Chicago Daily Tribune,* 1 May 1901: 6.
62. Anon. 1936a: 7.
63. O'Neill 1910a: 18.
64. Flinn 1887: 464. Police dates to this point are from Flinn 463-4.
65. Ffrench 1897: 113.
66. Brennan 1894: 15-16.
67. *Chicago Daily Tribune,* 30 Apr. 1901: 1.
68. Six times the salary of a patrolman, see O'Neill 1902: 23, 99-100.
69. *Chicago Daily Tribune,* 30 Apr. 1901: 1.
70. *Chicago Citizen,* 4 May 1901: 4. This estimate of O'Neill is typical of that of others. William Halley, author of a long-running newspaper series of profiles of the Chicago Irish, for instance, was of the same mind: 'Francis O'Neill... has attained his present position by sheer dint of hard work, intelligent execution of what is demanded of a police officer, united with good conduct, honor and integrity. He is a scholarly gentleman, fond of literature, music and art' (Halley 1904: 6).
71. *Chicago Citizen,* 1 May 1901: 6. It has been alleged that O'Neill owed his appointment to a Kate Doyle, at whose house O'Neill met weekly with three other policemen to play pipes, flute and fiddle, and who had once been the governess of Mayor Carter Harrison Junior, who first appointed him Chief (see Lindberg 1991: 53), but this is just someone's joke. I am obliged to Kevin Henry for bringing the Lindberg work to my attention and supplying extracts from it.
72. *Chicago Daily Tribune,* 30 Apr. 1901: 3.
73. Ibid.
74. *Chicago Citizen,* 21 Nov. 1903: 5.
75. O'Neill 1902: passim.
76. *Chicago Sunday Tribune,* 1 Sept. 1901: 1.
77. Lindberg 1991: 27, 53, 109.
78. Anon. 1901: 38.
79. Lindberg 1991: 73.
80. Currey 1912: 226.
81. Anon. 1936a: 7.
82. O'Neill quoted in Lindberg 1991: 53.
83. *Chicago Daily Tribune,* 25 July 1905: 1, 5.
84. O'Neill is also referred to in several independent sources as 'Colonel'. Whether this was an earned or honorary rank I have not been able to establish.
85. *Chicago Daily Tribune,* 25 July 1905: 1.
86. Ibid., 30 Apr. 1901: 1.
87. Anon. 1936a: 7.
88. Kipley's obituary in the *Chicago Citizen,* 13 Feb. 1904: 5, which describes O'Neill's visit to Kipley's deathbed:
    A touching scene of Kipley's last hours was his parting with Chief of Police O'Neill, his old friend and former subordinate, in the morning. Mr. Kipley extended his hand feebly, and Chief O'Neill grasped it. 'I know I am going to go, Frank', the veteran said. 'You were always a good officer and I always liked you. I am prepared to die. Good-by.'
89. Harrison 1944: 136.
90. O'Neill 1902: 5.
91. *Chicago Daily Tribune,* 6 Apr. 1905: 5. This source reports O'Neill as saying about the list of eligible appointees which included this policeman: 'I took them just as they came, regardless of nationality, color, or anything else.'
92. Goldman 1932, vol. 1: 300-2, 305, 308, 310-11:
    The same evening Chief of Police O'Neill came to my cell. He informed me that he would like to have a quiet talk with me. 'I have no wish to bully or coerce you', he said; 'perhaps I can help you'. 'It would indeed be a strange experience to have help from a chief of police', I replied; 'but I am quite willing to answer your questions'... When I had concluded – what I said being taken down in shorthand – Chief O'Neill remarked: 'Unless you're a very clever actress, you are certainly innocent. I think you are innocent, and I am going to do my part to help you out'. I was too amazed to thank him; I had never before heard such a tone from a police officer' (302).
    A friend of Goldman's thought that O'Neill, 'a shrewd Irishman', was using her in his war against corrupt policemen who had been using

the anarchist scare as a cover for their own activities (310-11). I am obliged to Peter Browne and Pearse Hutchinson for this reference.

93. Lindberg 1991: 53. The enquiry was headed by a Captain Piper. This complaint was also voiced by Edward Dunne when he was running for mayor against Carter Harrison in 1904 (Sullivan 1916: 163).

94. Lindberg 1991: 53, 230.

95. *Historical Encyclopaedia of Illinois*, Chicago 1920 ed., quoted in Anon. 1936a: 13.

96. The Irish-American Chicago writer Peter Finlay Dunne in one of his subtle dialect pieces of the 1890s indicates a connection in the popular mind between the Chicago police and Irish traditional music, and confirms a later observation of O'Neill's (see below) that a false refinement was causing some Irish immigrants to turn their backs on the music:

'Ol' man Donahue bought Molly a pianny las' week', Mr Dooley said... 'She'd been takin' lessons fr'm a Dutchman down th' sthreet, an' they say she can play as aisy with her hands crossed as she can with wan finger...' 'D'ye know "The Rambler fr'm Clare"?,' says Slavin. 'No,' says Molly. 'It goes like this,' says Slavin. 'A-ah, din yadden, yooden a-yadden, arrah yadden ay-a.' 'I dinnaw it,' says th' girl. 'Tis a low chune, annyhow,' says Mrs Donahue. 'Misther Slavin ividintly thinks he's at a polis picnic,' she says. 'I'll have no come-all-ye's in this house,' she says... 'If ye want to hear that kind iv chune, ye can go down to Finucane's Hall,' she says, 'an' call in Crowley, th' blind piper,' she says. 'Molly,' she says, 'give us wan iv thim Choochooski things,' she says. 'They're so ginteel.'

(*Chicago Evening Post*, 20 Apr. 1895, quoted in Fanning 1987: 144-5).

97. O'Neill 1910a: 31.

98. O'Neill 1910a: 217-8.

99. O'Neill 1910a: 216-7. The rumour circulated on 20 Feb. 1902 (*Chicago Daily Tribune*, 21 Feb. 1902: 1).

100. Letter from O'Neill to Ó Floinn, op. cit.

101. O'Neill 1973: vi.

102. Ffrench 1897: 314-5.

103. Blue Book 1902: 65 passim.

104. Ennis 1902: 37.

105. Halley 1904: 6.

106. *Chicago Citizen*, 17 Oct. 1904: 1.

107. *Chicago Citizen*, 1 Oct. 1904: 3.

108. Letter from O'Neill to John O'Neill, 16 June 1916. For Irish revolutionary movements in O'Neill's Chicago see Funchion 1976: passim. The chief of the violent Irish nationalist groups operating there in his time was Clan-na-Gael, whose members directed a dynamiting campaign against London from Chicago in the early 1880s.

109. Typescript of notes and comments dictated by O'Neill on the tunes in *The Dance Music of Ireland* (copy in Cnuasach an Bhreathnaigh, Irish Traditional Music Archive).

110. Some 30 of O'Neill's cylinders of Irish-American musicians, including Touhey and McFadden and Early, are in the archive of the Music Department, University College Cork (Mary Mitchell, pers. comm., Jan. 1995). For two others see Note 164.

111. Harry Bradshaw, pers. comm., June 1995.

112. O'Neill 1934a: 1, 13. I am obliged to Reg Hall for bringing this article to my attention and supplying me with a copy.

113. O'Neill 1913: 480.

114. Letter from O'Neill to Graves, op. cit.

115. Anon. 1905: 280.

116. Anon. 1936a: 7.

117. Griffin 1990: 184-5.

118. Letter from O'Neill to Ó Floinn, op. cit.

119. Ibid.

120. Letter from O'Neill to William Halpin, Co Clare, 27 Jan. 1914. Published in *An Píobaire*, 1st series, no 25 (Dec. 1975): 2.

121. Anon. 1905: 280.

122. Ibid.

123. *Chicago Citizen*, 20 Feb. 1904: 5.

124. Letter from O'Neill to Seamus Ó Casaide, 28 Aug. 1917 (National Library of Ireland MS 8116 (7)), and obituary of Rogers in the *Chicago Citizen*, 20 Feb. 1904: 5.

125. Letter from O'Neill to William Halpin, 8 November 1912.

126. Letter from O'Neill to John O'Neill, op. cit. (16 June 1916).

127. McCaffrey 1987: 7.

128. The daughters are named in a letter from F.H. Boland to Donal O'Sullivan, 14 Apr. 1949.

129. O'Neill 1910a: 288.

130. Ó Riabhaigh 1969a: 2-3.

131. See Notes 1 and 3.

132. *Cork Examiner*, 4 Aug. 1906: 4, and O'Neill 1910a: 70.

133. O'Neill 1910a: 121-3, 224, 228-9.

134. Graves 1907: 31. Graves, father of the poet and novelist Robert Graves, was one of the founders of the Irish Folk Song Society in London in 1903.

135. *Cork Examiner*, 23 July 1906: 6.

136. O'Neill 1907: 5 of Introduction.

137. O'Neill 1910a: 288.

138. Letter from O'Neill to William Halpin, 28 Dec. 1911. Published in *An Píobaire*, 1st series, no 16-17 (Apr. 1974): 3-4.

139. Letter from O'Neill to Ó Floinn, op. cit. O'Neill himself had all these qualities.

140. Ibid.

141. I take it that Delaney was married to a sister of Anna O'Neill.

142. O'Neill 1913: 396.

143. O'Neill 1913: 484.

144. His own words in O'Neill 1922: ix.

145. He was a member of the Cork Historical and Archaeological Society and made several contributions to its journal. He also belonged to the American Irish Historical Society, and addressed it in 1916 (letter from O'Neill to John O'Neill, 16 June 1916).

146. *Chicago Daily Tribune*, 25 July 1905: 1, 5.
147. Letter from O'Neill to John O'Neill, op. cit. (13 Nov. 1916).
148. Breandán Breathnach in Ó Conluain 1979.
149. Letter from O'Neill to Seamus Ó Casaide in Dublin, 15 Mar. 1935 (National Library of Ireland MS 10,688 (12)).
150. O'Neill's death certificate.
151. *Chicago Daily Tribune*, 3 Apr. 1901: 3. The house no longer exists, and the street is now part of the campus of the University of Chicago.
152. O'Neill's death certificate. The mausoleum had been erected after the death of Rogers in 1904 (Kevin Henry, pers. comm., Aug. 1995).
153. Anon. 1936a. An independent obituary appeared in the *New York Times* on 29 Jan. 1936.
154. Fielding 1934: 60, and University College Cork cylinders.
155. Letter from O'Neill to Ó Floinn, op. cit.
156. Letter from O'Neill to Seamus Ó Casaide, 7 June 1917 (National Library of Ireland MS 8116(7)).
157. Fielding 1934: 34. O'Neill said that one of the chief regrets of his life was having lost by early emigration the opportunity to learn the fiddle from Timothy Downing, who had started him on the flute (O'Neill 1913: 410).
158. Letter from O'Neill to Ó Casaide, op. cit. (28 Aug. 1917).
159. Letter from O'Neill to Ó Casaide, op. cit. (7 June 1917).
160. Fielding 1934: 34.
161. Ó Casaide 1913: 8.
162. Ó Riabhaigh 1969b: Programmes 2 and 3, and the *New Orleans Picayune* in a review of O'Neill 1903, quoted in the *Chicago Citizen* (16 Apr. 1904: 4): 'The author was one of the visitors at the convention of police chiefs held in New Orleans recently and was a prime favorite, always pleasant and ready to break into song when called upon.'
163. Graves 1907: 31.
164. Interview with Mary (May) O'Neill in *Chicago Sunday Times*, 16 Mar. 1981, quoted in Gershen 1989: 58, and Kevin Henry, pers. comm., Aug. 1995. Kevin's information had come from Theresa Geary, a musician and daughter of a piper friend of O'Neill's, who acted as an amanuensis in his later life. In the Folk Music Division of the Department of Irish Folklore, University College Dublin, there are disc dubs (nos 938b and 939b), made in 1949, of two Chicago-made cylinders, loaned by a relative of Fr Henebry, on which the music seems to be introduced by O'Neill and which seem to feature him playing 'The Fermoy Lasses' reel and 'The Boys of Bluehill' hornpipe on whistle in trio with [Edward] Cronin on fiddle and [Thomas] Kiley on banjo-mandolin (Jackie Small, pers. comm., June 1996). I am obliged to Ríonach uí Ógáin of the Department of Irish Folklore for making the recordings available to me for listening.
165. O'Neill 1910a: 16.
166. O'Neill 1910a: 17.
167. A report in the New York newspaper the *Irish World* of 16 November 1901, involving O'Neill's friend the professional piper Patsy Touhey, whose music frequently had the power to break through the surface of false respectability, records one such occasion:
Many people may think that purely Irish dances are not popular among the Irish people in this country, and while they might be right, still there is a large number with whom these dances are still what they were in the old land – a source of pleasure and enjoyment.
The Springfield Irish Language Society held one of these dances last Thursday evening, feeling they could at least clear expenses and nothing more, but they were treated to the biggest surprize they ever experienced for the committee had to entertain five hundred guests as best they could in small quarters. This was not hard as all that could find room danced to the music of the pipes of Mr. P. Touhey, the great Irish piper, and in connection with the pipes, or rather pipe music, it is a source of mystery to anyone who witness[es] its effect upon the Irishman how he ever allowed the pipes to die, or nearly so...
At this entertainment I saw men and women who did not have the opportunity of hearing the pipe music or of dancing these dances since they left the old land, and their enjoyment was unbounded on this occasion... The first part of the programme was given to a literary entertainment, which consisted of Irish and English songs and speeches, Irish step dancing and instrumental music. This part was curtailed, owing to the large attendance, the rest of the evening being given up to Irish jigs, reels, hornpipes and 'sets' as danced in Ireland...
168. O'Neill 1910a: 17.
169. O'Neill 1910a: 18-19. Patrick O'Mahony and Michael Keating may be among the Deering Street policemen pictured on page 14 above.
170. O'Neill 1910a: 24-5. Shea was famous in the city as chief of detectives. Before O'Neill retired in 1905, he bought a farm from him (*Chicago Daily Tribune*, 25 July 1905: 1).
171. O'Neill 1910a: 100.
172. O'Neill 1910a: 41-2.
173. O'Neill 1913: 289-95.
174. Letter from O'Neill to Ó Casaide, op. cit. (7 June 1917).
175. O'Neill 1910a: 29 where O'Neill says that he made the acquaintance of James shortly before he himself moved to police headquarters (1884), and O'Neill 1913: 396-7.
176. O'Neill 1913: 396. James O'Neill died in 1949.
177. Anon. 1903:8.
178. This paragraph is summarised from O'Neill 1913: 396-8. A music notebook of James O'Neill's begun in 1888 survives (Jim McGuire in Ó Conluain 1979), but it is not clear whether this was part of the collaborative project.

179. *Chicago Sunday Tribune,* 24 Aug. 1901: 38 which says that O'Neill had been seriously collecting for preservation for over a dozen years. The idea of publishing the music preserved was probably conceived in the 1890s.
180. O'Neill 1910a: 75.
181. O'Neill 1903: 4.
182. Anon. 1902: 53.
183. Typescript dictated by O'Neill, see Note 109 above.
184. Fielding 1934: 34-5.
185. *Chicago Citizen,* 9 Mar. 1901: 1.
186. 'Hints to Amateur Pipers' in O'Neill 1910a: 332-7. For a study of Touhey see Mitchell & Small 1986.
187. O'Neill 1910a: 65-6.
188. *Chicago Sunday Tribune,* 2 Mar. 1902: 53.
189. Most of O'Neill's own contribution consists of tunes from his childhood and later playing experience, but Breandán Breathnach has criticised him for also attributing to himself melodies taken from the Bunting and Petrie collections (Breathnach 1977b: 115). It is possible that O'Neill preferred their versions of tunes which he knew to his own versions, and therefore published theirs.
190. O'Neill 1907: 3 of Introduction.
191. O'Neill 1910a: 478. O'Neill himself was not the instigator although he cooperated at first.
192. Fielding 1934: 60.
193. Letter from O'Neill to Halpin, op. cit. (28 Dec. 1911).
194. O'Neill 1910a: 59.
195. Letter from O'Neill to Ó Floinn, op. cit. This is presumably the same incident referred to in O'Neill 1910a: 59. The implication seems to be that a gun was drawn, possibly by one of the policeman members.
196. Letter from O'Neill to William Halpin, 9 Mar. 1912. Published in *An Píobaire,* 1st series, no 18 (May 1974): 5.
197. Ennis 1901: 4.
198. O'Neill 1913: 118. 'Mary O'Neill's Fancy' (O'Neill 1903: 242) is named for a sister of James O'Neill, not for Francis's daughter of the same name (Letter from O'Neill to Graves, op. cit.).
199. O'Crowley n.d.: 44.
200. O'Neill does not name the offending member, but John Ennis, who wrote frequently on Irish music for the press, must be a candidate. His opinions, such as these which he expressed in the *Chicago Citizen,* 2 Mar. 1901: 1, were often less than moderate:
    The Irish people, after a long surfeit of London music hall rot, the operatic effusions of maniacs, and the alleged 'Negro melodies' that emanate from a few degenerate Irish-Americans and Hebrews in New York, have awakened to the fact that they have been led astray, and that their own old music (the decrees of fashion to the contrary not withstanding) surpasses in melody, expressiveness, sweetness and beauty that of any other the world has yet produced.

201. O'Neill 1910a: 54. Other sources (e.g. Anon. 1902: 53) state that the committee met regularly.
202. O'Neill 1910a: 55.
203. Anon. 1902: 53.
204. Ibid.
205. Letter from O'Neill to Bernard Bogue, 28 May 1917. I am obliged to Harry Bradshaw for a copy of this letter.
206. Anon. 1902: 53.
207. O'Neill 1910a: 53.
208. 'Only for one of the thousands of parts printed by him does O'Neill furnish a repeat...' (Breathnach 1977b: 115).
209. O'Neill 1924: 169. He made some attempts to indicate ornamentation, in the opening pages of O'Neill 1907, for example, but quickly abandoned them.
210. O'Neill 1910a: 55.
211. This is borne out by a letter of 1906 from O'Neill to Graves (op. cit.) where he writes about committing a tune to memory from a manuscript copy; by a letter he wrote to Bogue in 1917 (op. cit.) where he talks about 'looking over and playing the tunes you so kindly sent me', but admits that his skill in notation 'is limited – scientifically speaking'; by his claim to have noted a tune from performance (O'Neill 1924: 164); and by his daughter's reference to him writing music from his own playing (see Note 164 above). His basic music literacy is also indicated by his references to tunes in the notes to O'Neill 1924, and by what seem to be his personal markings on music manuscripts (Fuderer 1990: 2). Ó Riabhaigh 1969b: Programme 3 claims that O'Neill was collecting music on paper in America long before he came to Chicago, but this contradicts O'Neill's own testimony (1910a: passim) where he constantly talks about 'memorising' tunes. His acute ear and retentive musical memory, and the scribal abilities of James O'Neill and others, reduced his need to write or read music.
212. Letter from O'Neill to Graves, op. cit.
213. Jackie Small has estimated that some 16% of the Ryan tunes are also found in O'Neill, although not necessarily in identical versions (pers. comm., Oct. 1992). Pat Sky has written an MA thesis on Ryan's collection: *Elias Howe and William Bradbury Ryan, Producers of Ryan's Mammoth Collection,* University of North Carolina at Chapel Hill, 1993; I am obliged to him for a copy. The Ryan volume was republished in 1995, with an introduction by Pat Sky, by the Mel Bay Co. of Missouri.
214. O'Neill 1910a: 113.
215. The second version of the double jig 'The Hare in the Corn' in O'Neill 1903: 143, which he says was taken by him from 'an American collection' (O'Neill 1910a: 159), is identical with the version in Ryan 1883. Ryan is in his library list of 1919, see Note 28.
216. It may also be, of course, that he and Ryan borrowed from some of the same older sources. At

any rate, O'Neill did not take the earlier volume into account in 1922 when he was calculating the number of Irish dance tunes preserved by other collectors (O'Neill 1922: viii), even though it contains several hundred such tunes.

217. Title-page.

218. Lyon and Healy, which claimed to be the largest music firm in the world, and which produced almost all of O'Neill's works, was co-founded in 1864 by Patrick Joseph Healy, also an immigrant from Co. Cork (Dolge 1911: 350).

219. Anon. 1903:8.

220. Note by Breandán Breathnach in Cnuasach an Bhreathnaigh, Irish Traditional Music Archive, attributing the information to a 'letter [from O'Neill] to Jennings, Deirdre Tobin's grandfather'. Jennings was an inspector of police in Waterford.

221. O'Neill 1910a: 57.

222. O'Neill 1903: Dedication.

223. See advertisements in O'Neill 1908. O'Neill's publications normally carry advertisements for each other.

224. Letter from O'Neill to Bogue, op. cit.

225. O'Neill 1907: inside back cover.

226. O'Neill 1907: 3.

227. See for instance the issue of 12 Mar. 1904: 1. The previous year the paper had attacked O'Neill's friend Fr Fielding for his views on the Royal Irish Constabulary, and said that Fielding had alleged in a 1903 lecture that 'when Irishmen able to play the pipes, or the fiddle, or the flute arrived in Chicago, situations were provided for them – generally by Mr O'Neill, in the police force' (issue of 28 Nov. 1903: 5). The ebullient Fielding had indeed said something to this effect in a speech delivered in the Rotunda in Dublin which was reported in various places including the *Chicago Citizen*, 19 Dec. 1903: 1. This source made its own contribution to the growing story about the permeation of the force by Irish traditional musicians with a sub-heading 'One hundred Irish pipers in the Chicago police force'.

228. Henebry 1903: 11, 29-30.

229. Issue of 27 Feb. 1904: 1.

230. New Series, vol. 23, no 4 (Apr. 1904): 150.

231. Ibid., no 5 (May 1904): 196.

232. Issue of 2 Apr. 1904. His charges, which he admitted were based on the first 300 tunes in the collection, were challenged in the same periodical by the Rev. Heinrich Bewerunge, then professor of Sacred Music at St Patrick's College, Maynooth, who was clearly sympathetic to O'Neill (issue of 23 Apr. 1904: 6). I am obliged to Seán Donnelly for bringing these sources to my attention.

233. Lecture reported in the *Cork Constitution*, 13 Oct. 1905: [3], and *The Leader*, 22 Oct. 1905: 140-1.

234. O'Neill 1910a: 56. Watergrass Hill is north of Cork city.

235. O'Neill 1910a: 80.

236. Letter from O'Neill to Bogue, op. cit. Breathnach 1977b: 115 states that it includes 185 new tunes,

that 24 settings and 72 key signatures were changed, and that 254 other minor alterations were made in the music notation.

237. Breathnach 1960: 13.

238. The first and second 'editions' were most likely two destroyed printings, see following note.

239. Letter from O'Neill to Ó Casaide, op. cit. (7 June 1917); letter from O'Neill to Bogue, op. cit. The latter speaks of one 'edition' of 1,000 copies being destroyed due to Edward Cronin's errors, and a second to James O'Neill's.

240. Letter from O'Neill to Ó Casaide, op. cit. (7 June 1917).

241. Letter from O'Neill to Bogue, op. cit.

242. Caitlín Uí Éigeartaigh, pers. comm., July 1996. I am obliged to Caitlín for analysing for me the piano arrangements of James and Selena O'Neill.

243. By W.H. Grattan Flood for one, in Brown 1912: 131. He thought them 'unmusicianly'.

244. O'Neill 1910a: Preface. This series does not appear to have been published.

245. Anon. 1911: 21.

246. Born about 1893 according to O'Neill 1910a: 60, but in 1899 according to ASCAP 1966: 550.

247. Letter from O'Neill to John O'Neill, op. cit. (13 Nov. 1916), and O'Neill 1913: 405.

248. Letter from O'Neill to John O'Neill, op. cit. (13 Nov. 1916).

249. Letter from O'Neill to Bogue, op. cit. I have heard it said – by whom I do not remember – that O'Neill was involved in setting up these and other Victor Chicago recordings of Irish music in 1928.

250. Caitlín Uí Éigeartaigh, pers. comm., July 1996.

251. Letter from O'Neill used as frontispiece in her 1940 reprint of O'Neill 1907.

252. Title-page.

253. Front inside cover.

254. O'Neill 1913: Preface.

255. Breandán Breathnach in Ó Conluain 1979.

256. Letter from O'Neill to William Halpin, 30 Dec. 1913.

257. Programme 1913: [2].

258. O'Neill 1913: passim.

259. O'Neill 1915: Foreword to enlarged edition.

260. Letter from O'Neill to Bogue, op. cit.

261. 'Being now some years since I have heard any Irish music, memory is no longer acute. Most of our musicians of the old school are old or dead.' (Letter of 1917 from O'Neill to Bogue, op. cit.).

262. O'Neill 1915: Foreword to enlarged edition.

263. Letter to Ó Floinn, op. cit.

264. O'Neill 1922: ix.

265. It was published on 18 Nov. 1922 and received in the Library of Congress for copyright registration on 29 November 1922 (copyright registration card, Library of Congress, Washington D.C.). I am obliged to Joe Hickerson of the Library's Archive of Folk Culture for guiding me through the copyright records, 'the largest collection of file cards in the world'.

266. Copy in the National Library of Ireland presented by O'Neill to W.H. Grattan Flood. The dedication,

in O'Neill's hand, is dated 22 Nov. 1924, and Grattan Flood, who was a friend and correspondent of O'Neill's and whom O'Neill admired, is likely to have one of the first to have received a presentation copy. The few other library copies I have found have accession dates later than 1924, if any. It must, however, be noticed that O'Neill's letter of 3 Jan. 1924 to Selena O'Neill (see Note 251) seems to imply that he was finished publishing at the beginning of 1924.

267. As early as 1925, O'Neill was complaining to W.H. Grattan Flood in Enniscorthy that he was nearly blind from cataracts (letter of 3 Jan. 1925 pasted in National Library of Ireland copy of O'Neill 1924).

268. Letter from O'Neill to Fr Charles L. O'Donnell, president of Notre Dame University, 29 Sept. 1931 (Dept of Special Collections, Hesburgh Library, Notre Dame University).

269. Anon. 1901: 38.

270. I was pleased and surprised to be presented with a mint copy of *Irish Minstrels and Musicians* for the Irish Traditional Music Archive, still sealed in paper as it had come from the printer in 1913, by Mr John Lesch, a relative of Francis O'Neill's, during the Milwaukee Irish Fest Summer School of August 1995. The copy has been used as a source of illustrations for this work.

271. Letter from Paul R. Byrne, Director of Libraries, University of Notre Dame, Indiana, to John M. Conway, Irish Consul in Chicago, n.d. but c. 1949 (Dept of Special Collections, Hesburgh Library, Notre Dame University). Sergeant James Early of Chicago and Fire Captain Michael Dunn of Milwaukee were two who received O'Neill material (Jim McGuire in Ó Conluain 1979).

272. Jim McGuire in Ó Conluain 1979. See also Mitchell & Small 1986: 10.

273. Undated clipping of c. 1980s from unknown Chicago newspaper in Archive of Folk Culture, Library of Congress, Washington D.C.

274. Breandán Breathnach, pers. comm., 1984.

275. Harry Bradshaw, pers. comm., Oct. 1993.

276. Mary (May) O'Neill in the *Chicago Sunday Times*, 16 Mar. 1981, quoted in Gershen 1989: 58.

277. 'Philadelphia' was one such (letter from O'Neill to John O'Neill, op. cit.: 16 June 1916).

278. See Note 112.

279. Jim McGuire in Ó Conluain 1979. O'Neill told Shannon that he was the best left-handed piper since Patsy Touhey.

280. Ed Reavy Jnr, pers. comm., June 1996.

281. See for instance O'Neill 1934: 25-26.

282. Fielding 1934: 60. The gesture was misunderstood, see Note 230.

283. Letter from O'Neill to Bogue, op. cit.

284. O'Neill 1913: 475.

285. See Breathnach 1977: 111 for a discussion.

286. See O'Neill 1911: 16-20.

287. O'Neill 1907: 3.

288. Carson 1986: 20.

289. O'Neill 1910a: 293-5.

290. Breathnach 1977: 118.

291. Letter from O'Neill to Ó Casaide, op. cit. (7 June 1917).

292. Brosnan 1979: 26.

293. Gershen 1989: 51. .

294. Moloney 1975: 16.

295. This unpublished index is in the Irish Traditional Music Archive, Dublin.

296. Anon 1936a: 7.

297. Paddy Murphy quoted in Ó hAllmhuráin 1993: 41.

298. In preparation by Liz Doherty and Paul McGettrick for Ossian Publications, Cork.

299. More than 35,000 copies have been sold of the Collins, later Rockchapel, reprint of O'Neill 1903 alone (Daniel Michael Collins, pers. comm, June 1996).

300. *An Píobaire*, Series 1, no 29, Dublin (Mar. 1977): [7].

301. Jim McGuire of Chicago, Sean V. Golden of Notre Dame University, Indiana, Michael Grainger of Cork, and Barry O'Neill of the University of Michigan were among those who supplied Breathnach with information (Breathnach 1977: Notes).

302. See Appendix.

303. *Treoir* vol. 10, no 2 (1978): 25.

304. Ibid., vol. 9, no 4 (Oct. 1977): 14.

305. Letter from Rev. Charles L. O'Donnell, president of Notre Dame, to O'Neill, 2 Oct. 1931 (Dept of Special Collections, Hesburgh Library, Notre Dame University).

306. Fuderer 1990: 1.

307. See Fuderer 1990.

308. In the hopes of finding hitherto unnoticed printings of O'Neill's various volumes, I give a breakdown of their pagination in each case.

309. 'Facsimile' in this Appendix can signify 'near-facsimile' as minor changes are often made to an original, especially in introductory matter.

310. What seems to be the first hardback edition was printed by Rayner, Dalheim & Co, music printers in Chicago, and contains three pages of photos of O'Neill's Chicago musician friends. Another hardback edition, printed by H.S. Talbot & Co, music engravers and printers, Chicago, has two pages of photos of Irish-based musicians. In the library of Trinity College Dublin there is a paperback edition 'engraved and printed' by Talbot with 'third edition' printed on the front cover only and the two pages of photos of the Irish-based musicians. In the library of the Music Division of the Department of Irish Folklore, University College Dublin, there is a paperback edition with the same photos which is marked 'fourth edition', again printed by Talbot. All these items are published by Lyon and Healy and dated 1907. It is my impression that there never was a second edition of the work, but that O'Neill took advantage of the need for a new printing to change printers and correct errors that remained after the scrapping of the first two printings (which he privately described as 'editions': see Notes 238 and 239), and eventually called the result the 'third edition'.

INFORMATION SOURCES

PERSONAL COMMUNICATIONS

As detailed in Notes from Harry Bradshaw, the late Breandán Breathnach, Daniel Michael Collins, Kevin Henry, Mary Mitchell, Catherine Mulhall, Fr Michael O'Donovan, Ed Reavy Jr, Jackie Small, and Caitlín Uí Éigeartaigh.

MANUSCRIPTS, TYPESCRIPTS

Baptismal register of 1840s, Caheragh Parish, Co. Cork
Death certificate of Francis O'Neill, Bureau of Vital Statistics, Chicago: cert. no 2829
Letters from Francis O'Neill, Chicago, to
- Bernard Bogue, Monaghan/Tyrone
- W.H. Grattan Flood, Enniscorthy, Co. Wexford
- A.P. Graves, Dublin/London
- William Halpin, Newmarket-on-Fergus, Co. Clare
- Séamus Ó Casaide, Dublin
- Rev. Charles L. O'Donnell, Notre Dame University, Indiana
- Rev. Séamus Ó Floinn, Cork
- John O'Neill, Cork
Francis O'Neill, typescript notes on tunes in O'Neill 1907
Francis O'Neill, typescript list of personal library, 1919
Letters from F.H. Boland, Dept of External Affairs, Dublin, to Donal O'Sullivan, Dublin
Letter from Paul R. Byrne, Notre Dame University, Indiana, to John M. Conway, Irish Consulate, Chicago
Letters from Rev. Charles L. O'Donnell, Notre Dame University, Indiana, to Francis O'Neill, Chicago
Charles S. Winslow, *Biographical Sketches of Chicagoians* vol. IV, typescript in Chicago Public Library, 1948: 1927-45

THESES

Gershen 1989   Paulette Gershen, *Francis O'Neill, Collector of Irish Music: A Biography*, senior thesis, Department of Folklore, University of California at Los Angeles, 1989
McCullough 1978   Lawrence E. McCullough, *Irish Music in Chicago: An Ethnomusicological Study*, Ph.D. thesis, University of Pittsburgh, 1978
Moloney 1992   Michael Moloney, *Irish Music in America: Continuity and Change*, Ph.D. thesis, University of Pennsylvania, 1992
Sky 1993   Patrick Sky, *Elias Howe and William Bradbury Ryan, Producers of* Ryan's Mammoth Collection, MA thesis, University of North Carolina at Chapel Hill, 1993

PERIODICALS

An Claidheamh Soluis, Dublin
An Gaodhal (The Gael), New York
An Píobaire, Dublin
Journal of the Cork Historical and Archaeological Society, Cork
Journal of the Irish Folk Song Society, London
Keystone Folklore, Pennsylvania
The Catholic Bulletin, Dublin
The Chicago Citizen, Chicago
The Chicago Daily Tribune, Chicago
The Chicago Sunday Times, Chicago
The Chicago Sunday Tribune, Chicago
The Cork Constitution, Cork

The Cork Examiner, Cork
The Cork Holly Bough, Cork
The Cork Weekly Examiner, Cork
The Evening Telegraph, Dublin
The Illustrated London News, London
The Irish Book Lover, Dublin
The Irish Independent, Dublin
The Irish World, New York
The Leader, Dublin
The New York Times, New York
The Southern Star, Skibbereen
The United Irishman, Dublin
Treoir, Dublin

ARTICLES, BOOKS, PROGRAMMES

Andreas 1886   A.T. Andreas, *History of Chicago from the Earliest Period to the Present Times* vol. 3, Chicago 1886

Anon. 1901   Anon., 'Francis O'Neill', *The Chicago Daily Tribune*, 25 Aug. 1901: 38

Anon. 1902   Anon., 'Chicago leads Ireland as storehouse of Irish music', *The Chicago Sunday Tribune*, 2 Mar. 1902: 53

Anon. 1903   Anon., 'Chief O'Neill an author', *The Chicago Daily Tribune*, 9 Aug. 1903: 8

Anon. 1905   Anon., 'Francis O'Neill', *Centennial History of the City of Chicago*, Its Men and Institutions. Biographical Sketches of Leading Citizens, Chicago 1905: 278-80

Anon. 1911   Anon., 'A collector's book', *Journal of the Irish Folk Song Society* vol. 9, no 1 (Jan. 1911): 21-2

Anon. 1936a   Anon., 'Chief of the Chicago police. Death of distinguished Bantry man. Roamer, author and musician...', *The Southern Star*, 8 Feb. 1936: 7, 13 (reprinted from a Chicago newspaper which I have not yet been able to identify). Reprinted in *The Irish Book Lover* vol. 29 no 3 (Dec. 1944): 2-6. A slightly edited version appeared in *The Irish Independent*, 31 Jan. 1936: 9, and other obituaries summarise it.

Anon. 1936b   Anon., 'From the hill tops', *The Catholic Bulletin* vol. XXVI, no 3 (Mar. 1936): 203-4

ASCAP 1966   *The ASCAP Biographical Dictionary of Composers, Authors and Publishers* [3rd ed.], New York 1966

Blessing 1980   Patrick J. Blessing, 'Irish', *Harvard Encyclopedia of American Ethnic Groups*, Stephan Thernstrom ed., Cambridge, Mass., 1980: 524-45

Blue Book 1902   *Blue Book of Cook County Democracy*, Chicago 1902

Breathnach 1960   Breandán Breathnach, 'Ceol damhsa', *Feasta* vol. 13, no 2 (May 1960): 13-4

Breathnach 1971   Breandán Breathnach, *Folk Music & Dances of Ireland*, Dublin 1971

Breathnach 1976a   Breandán Breathnach, 'Proinsias Ó Néill, bailitheoir ceoil Éireann', *Léachtaí Cholm Cille* vol. 7, 'An ceol i litríocht na Gaeilge' (1976): 149-66

Breathnach 1976b   Breandán Breathnach, 'In black and white', *Slow Air* vol. 1, no 2 (June 1976): 8-9

Breathnach 1977a   Breandán Breathnach, *Folk Music & Dances of Ireland* rev. ed., Dublin 1977

Breathnach 1977b   Breandán Breathnach, 'Francis O'Neill, collector of Irish music', *Dal gCais* vol. 7, Miltown Malbay, Co. Clare (1977): 112-19. Reprinted as in Appendix above.

Brennan 1894   [Michael Brennan], *Report of the General Superintendent of Police of the City of Chicago to the City Council for the Fiscal Year Ending December 31, 1894*, Chicago 1894

Brosnan 1979   John Joe Brosnan, 'Is it in the Book?', *Treoir* vol. 11, no 1 (1979): 26

Brown 1912   Stephen J. Brown, *A Guide to Books on Ireland* Part 1, Dublin 1912

Carson 1986   Ciaran Carson, *Pocket Guide to Irish Traditional Music*, Belfast 1986

Craoibhín 1937   An Craoibhín Aoibhinn [Douglas Hyde], *Mo Thuras go hAmerice*, Dublin 1937

Currey 1912   J. Seymour Currey, *Chicago: Its History and Its Builders* vol. 3, Chicago 1912

Dedmon 1981   Emmett Dedmon, *Fabulous Chicago* rev. ed., New York 1981

Dolge 1911   Alfred Dolge, *Pianos and Their Makers*, California 1911

Donnelly 1993   Seán Donnelly, 'Francis O'Neill and "The Fox Chase": a tale of two Touheys', *Ceol na hÉireann. Irish Music* vol. 1, Dublin 1993, pp. 55-62

Ennis 1901   John Ennis, 'Reception to Chief O'Neill', *The Chicago Citizen*, 1 June 1901: 4

Ennis 1902   Thomas Ennis, 'Irish pipes and pipers', *An Gaodhal (The Gael)*, New Series, vol. 21, no 2 (Feb. 1902): 31-8

Fanning 1987   Charles Fanning ed., *Mr Dooley and the Chicago Irish: The Autobiography of a Nineteenth-Century Ethnic Group*, Washington D.C., 1987

Ffrench 1897   Charles Ffrench, *Biographical History of the American Irish in Chicago*, Chicago 1897

Fielding 1934   Rev. James K. Fielding, *The Resurrection of a Nation*, Chicago 1934

Flinn 1887   John J. Flinn, *History of the Chicago Police*, Chicago 1887

Fuderer 1990   Laura Sue Fuderer, *Music Mad. Captain Francis O'Neill and Traditional Irish Music. An Exhibition from the Captain Francis O'Neill Collection of Irish Music, March 1990 - August 1990*, Department of Special Collections, University Libraries, University of Notre Dame, Indiana, 1990

Funchion 1976   Michael F. Funchion, *Chicago's Irish Nationalists 1881-1890*, New York 1976

Goldman 1932   Emma Goldman, *Living My Life* vols 1-2, London 1932

Graves 1907   A.P. Graves, 'Francis O'Neill's "Music of Ireland"', *Journal of the Irish Folk Song Society* vol. 5 (London 1907): 31-6

Griffin 1990   William D. Griffin, *The Book of Irish Americans*, New York 1990

Griffith 1853   Richard Griffith, *General Valuation of Rateable Property in Ireland... County of Cork. Barony of West Carbery (West Division), Unions of Bantry, Skull, and Skibbereen*, Dublin 1853

Halley 1904   William Halley, 'Topics of an old-timer (Second Series). The Irish in Chicago, pt XXI', *The Chicago Citizen*, 11 June 1904: 6

Harrison 1944   Carter H. Harrison, *Growing Up with Chicago*, Chicago 1944

Harrison 1992   Richard S. Harrison, *Bantry in Olden Days*, Bantry 1992

Henebry 1903   Richard Henebry, *Irish Music: Being an Examination of the Matter of Scales, Modes, and Keys, with Practical Instructions and Examples for Players*, Dublin 1903

Hickey 1995   Patrick Hickey, 'The Famine in the Skibbereen Union (1845-51)', *The Great Irish Famine*, Cathal Póirtéir ed., Cork 1995: 185-203

Hourihan 1977   J. Kevin Hourihan, 'Town Growth in West Cork: Bantry, 1600-1960', *Journal of the Cork Historical and Archaeological Society* vol. 82, no 236 (Jul. - Dec. 1977): 92-6

Kelly 1913   John Kelly, 'Writes history of Irish music. Francis O'Neill, former police chief, publishes new volume.', *The Chicago Daily Tribune,* 27 Oct. 1913: 8

Lindberg 1991   Richard C. Lindberg, *To Serve and Collect: Chicago Politics and Police Corruption from the Lager Beer Riot to the Summerdale Scandal,* Praeger, New York etc. 1991

McCaffrey 1987   Lawrence J. McCaffrey, 'The Irish-American dimension', *The Irish in Chicago,* L.J. McCaffrey et al. ed., Chicago 1987

McGuire 1980   Jim McGuire, 'Francis O'Neill and "The Book"', *Come for to Sing* vol. 6, no 1 (Winter 1980): 12-14

Mitchell & Small 1986 Pat Mitchell & Jackie Small, *The Piping of Patsy Touhey,* Dublin 1986

Moloney 1975   Michael Moloney, 'Medicine for life: a study of a folk composer and his music', *Keystone Folklore* nos 1-2 (Winter-Spring 1975): 5-37

Nic Craith 1993   Máiréad Nic Craith, *Malartú Teanga: An Ghaeilge i gCorcaigh sa Naoú hAois Déag,* Bremen 1993

O'Brien 1904   Patrick 'Rocky Mountain' O'Brien, *Birth and Adoption. A Book of Prose and Poetry,* New York 1904

Ó Casaide 1913   S. Ó C. [Séamus Ó Casaide], 'Irish Minstrels and Musicians. Chief O'Neill's new book', *Evening Telegraph,* 20 Dec. 1913: 8

O'Crowley n.d.   Tadhg O'Crowley, *Crowley's Collection of Music for the Highland or Irish Bagpipes* Book 1, Cork n.d. [but post Oct. 1936]

O'Donoghue n.d.   Bruno O'Donoghue, *Parish Histories and Place Names of West Cork,* Tralee n.d. [c.1986]

O'Flaherty 1927   Liam O'Flaherty, *The Life of Tim Healy,* London 1927

Ó hAllmhuráin 1993   Gearóid Ó hAllmhuráin, 'From Hughdie's to the Latin Quarter', *Treoir* vol. 25, no 2 (1993): 40-4

Ó Laoghaire 1986   Donnchadh Ó Laoghaire, 'Tralibane and Francis O'Neill', *Treoir* vol. 18, no 1 (1986): 7

Ó Mathghamhna 1974 Daithí Ó Mathghamhna, 'Septs of the O'Mahonys', *The O'Mahony Journal* vol. 4 (July 1974): 3-4

O'Neill 1902   [Francis O'Neill], *Report of the General Superintendent of Police of the City of Chicago to the City Council for the Fiscal Year Ending December 31, 1901,* Chicago 1902

O'Neill 1903   Francis O'Neill ed., *O'Neill's Music of Ireland,* Chicago 1903

O'Neill 1907   Francis O'Neill ed., *The Dance Music of Ireland,* Chicago 1907

O'Neill 1908   Francis O'Neill ed., *O'Neill's Irish Music. 250 Choice Selections,* Chicago 1908

O'Neill 1910a   Francis O'Neill, *Irish Folk Music: A Fascinating Hobby,* Chicago 1910

O'Neill 1910b   [Francis O'Neill ed.,] *Popular Selections from O'Neill's Dance Music of Ireland,* Chicago 1910

O'Neill 1911   Francis O'Neill, 'Enthusiasm and Irish folk song', *Journal of the Irish Folk Song Society* vol. 10 (1911): 16-20

O'Neill 1913   Francis O'Neill, *Irish Minstrels and Musicians,* Chicago 1913

O'Neill 1915   Francis O'Neill ed., *O'Neill's Irish Music. 400 Choice Selections,* Chicago 1915

O'Neill 1922   Francis O'Neill ed., *Waifs and Strays of Gaelic Melody* 1st ed., Chicago 1922

O'Neill 1924   Francis O'Neill ed., *Waifs and Strays of Gaelic Melody* 2nd ed., Chicago 1922 [recte 1924]

O'Neill 1934a   Francis O'Neill, 'Irish dances and dance-music', *The Cork Weekly Examiner* (7 Apr. 1934): 1, 13

O'Neill 1934b   Francis O'Neill, 'Irish music' in festival programme *The Pageant of the Celt,* Mathias J. Harford ed., Chicago, 28-29 August 1934

O'Neill 1973a   Barry O'Neill, 'Introduction to the reprint edition' in Francis O'Neill, *Irish Folk Music: A Fascinating Hobby,* Darby, Pennsylvannia, 1973 reprint of O'Neill 1910

O'Neill 1973b   Barry O'Neill, 'Introduction to the reprint edition' in Francis O'Neill, *Irish Minstrels and Musicians,* Darby, Pennsylvannia, 1973 reprint of O'Neill 1913

Ó Riabhaigh 1962   Micheál Ó Riabhaigh, 'Captain Francis O'Neill – collector of Irish music', *The Cork Holly Bough* (1962): 34-5

Ó Riabhaigh 1969a   Micheál Ó Riabhaigh, 'Cumann na bPíobairí Uilleann, Corcaigh', *An Píobaire* Series 1, no 1 (Mar. 1969): 2-3

Programme 1913   Festival programme: *Feis under Auspices of Gaelic League of Ireland, Comiskey Park, Aug. 3, 1913,* Chicago 1913

Rehm 1874   [Jacob Rehm,] *Report of the Board of Police, in the Police Department, to the Common Council of the City of Chicago for the Year Ending March 31, 1874,* Chicago 1874

Ryan 1883   [William Bradbury Ryan,] *Ryan's Mammoth Collection. 1050 Reels and Jigs, Hornpipes, Clogs...,* Boston 1883

Smith 1994   Graeme Smith, 'My love is in America: migration and Irish music', *The Creative Migrant (Irish World Wide Series* vol. 3), Patrick O'Sullivan ed., Leicester etc. 1994

Sullivan 1916   William L Sullivan ed., *Dunne: Judge, Mayor, Governor,* Chicago 1916

SOUND RECORDINGS

O'Neill/Henebry cylinders in archive of Music Dept, University College Cork

Disc dubs of two cylinders, Dept of Irish Folklore, University College Dublin: nos 938b and 939b

Commercial disc: Michael Coleman, 'The Grey Goose', Columbia 33237-F, New York 1927

RADIO PROGRAMMES

Carson 1981   'Chief O'Neill's Favourites', 30 min. radio programme written by Ciaran Carson, produced by Paul Muldoon, transmitted BBC Radio Ulster, 1981

Browne 1988   'Airneán' series special programme on Francis O'Neill, written, presented and produced by Peter Browne, transmitted RTÉ Radio 1, 31 Jan. 1988

Ó Conluain 1979   'The Captain from Chicago and His "Fascinating Hobby"'', 30 min. radio programme written, presented and produced by Proinsias Ó Conluain, transmitted RTÉ Radio 1, 29 Aug. 1979

Ó Riabhaigh 1969b   'Francis O'Neill and Irish Music', six 15 min. radio programmes written and presented by Micheál Ó Riabhaigh, produced by Ciarán Mac Mathúna, transmitted Radió Éireann, Dublin, 11 Sept. - 16 Oct. 1969

MUSIC NOTATIONS, DRAWINGS, PHOTOGRAPHS

All printed music notations are from O'Neill 1903 except those on pages 19 (O'Neill 1907), 25 (O'Neill 1913), 40 (Tadhg O'Crowley, *Crowley's Collection of Music for the Highland or Irish Bagpipes,* Book 1, Cork n.d. [post Oct. 1936], reproduced courtesy of Crowley's Music Shop, McCurtain St, Cork), 47 (O'Neill 1908), and 48 (O'Neill 1910b).

Sources for manuscript music notations, drawings, and photographs are in Picture Credits below.

Quotations in captions to pictures are from O'Neill 1910a or O'Neill 1913, where they will be found through the indexes, except those on pages 5 (*Illustrated London News,* 20 Feb. 1847: 116) and 20 (letter from Francis to John O'Neill, Cork, 16 June 1916).

PICTURE CREDITS

Pictures, excluding printed music, are reproduced by courtesy of the following institutions and individuals (numbering from page left to right and top to bottom):

Bantry Historical Society: 9a
Harry Bradshaw, Dublin: 57b
Chicago Historical Society: Front cover background, back cover, 12a, 12c, 14b, 15a, 16c-d, 18b, 20a
Laura Sue Fuderer, Notre Dame Libraries, Indiana: 52b, 60a-b
Reg Hall, London: 54a
Irish Traditional Music Archive, Dublin: Frontispiece, 21b, 22a, 25a-b, 26a-c, 27b, 29a, 30a, 31a, 33b, 34b, 35a-b, 37a-b, 38a-c, 39a-c, 40b, 41a, 44a-c, 45a, 46a-b, 47a-c, 48a-b, 49a-c, 50a-c, 51b-c, 52a, 53a-b, 56a, 56c, 57c, 58b, 60c
Irish Vincentian Archives, Dublin: 45b
Pier Kuipers, Dublin: 4a, 10a-b
John Loesberg, Cork: 24a
Jim McGuire, Chicago: 28b
Liam McNulty, Dublin: 56b
Mulligan Records, Dublin: 58c
Máirtín O'Connor: 58d
Aidan O'Hara, Dublin: 54b
Mrs Máire Ó Máirtín, Cork (photographs by the late Dónal Ó Máirtín): 58e, 59a
Willie Clancy Summer School, Clare: 57a
Ian Vickery, photographer, Bantry: 6a

ACKNOWLEDGEMENTS

My thanks are due in the first instance to John Loesberg of Ossian Publications for his invitation to write an introduction to Francis O'Neill for his forthcoming edition of O'Neill's music collections. Neither of us expected that it would grow to anything of the present size, but it has, in odd hours on trains and planes, or while waiting for rush-hour traffic to subside, and in the crevices between other work. John has taken the result cheerfully and has kindly proposed this separate publication.

I am especially obliged to Harry Bradshaw for discussing various aspects of O'Neill with me and for making illustrations and other information sources available, as detailed in the Notes; to Pier Kuipers for his care and skill with design; and, as always, to Maeve Carolan for advice and support. My thanks also for information and other personal help to Peter Browne, Kitty Buckley, Tim Cadogan, Ciaran Carson, Daniel Michael Collins, Glenn Cumiskey, Helen Davies, Siobhán de hÓir, Seán Donnelly, Laura Sue Fuderer, Paulette Gershen, Reg Hall, Colin Hamilton, Kevin Henry, Joe Hickerson, Pearse Hutchinson, Phil Jones, Maire Kennedy, Ian Lee, John Lesch, Christopher Lynch, Jim McGuire, Dermot McLaughlin, Liam McNulty and Na Píobairí Uilleann, Mary Mitchell, Mick Moloney, Catherine Mulhall, Tom Munnelly, Sadhbh Nic Ionnraic, Treasa Ní Earcáin, Íde Ní Thuama, Bill Ochs, Proinsias Ó Conluain, Fr Patrick O'Donoghue and the Irish Vincentian Archives, Fr Michael O'Donovan, Kate O'Dwyer, Aidan O'Hara, Máire Ó Máirtín, Séamus Ó Néill and Mulligan Records, Siobhán O'Rafferty, Kathleen O'Riordan, Muiris Ó Rócháin and the Willie Clancy Summer School, Clíona O'Sullivan, Fr Ted O'Sullivan, Ena Phelan, Noel Rice, Hugh Shields, Pat Sky, Jim Sloan, Jackie Small, Malcolm Taylor, Caitlín Uí Éigeartaigh, Ríonach uí Ógáin, Ian Vickery, Ormonde Waters, and Penny Woods. I am also obliged to the organisers of the Milwaukee Irish Fest 1995 Summer School and the Bantry Bay '96 Summer School whose invitations to lecture enabled me to pursue researches in Chicago and Tralibane.

I am grateful also to the staffs of several libraries and institutions: in Dublin the National Library of Ireland, the Gilbert Library, Trinity College Library, and the libraries of the Royal Society of Antiquaries of Ireland, the Royal Irish Academy, the Irish Architectural Archive, and the Folk Music Division of the Department of Irish Folklore, University College Dublin; in Belfast the Belfast Central Library; in Bantry the Bantry Historical Society and Bantry Public Library; in Cork the Music Department of University College Cork; in London the British Library and the Vaughan Williams Memorial Library; in the United States the New York Public Library, the library of the American Irish Historical Society in New York, the Boston Public Library, the Library of Congress, the library of the Chicago Historical Society, the Newberry Library of Chicago, the Chicago Public Library (Harold Washington Library Center), the Department of Special Collections of the Hesburgh Library in the University of Notre Dame, Indiana, the Music Library of the University of Illinois at Urbana-Champaign, and the John Jermain Memorial Library of Sag Harbor, New York. Thanks also to those libraries which make their catalogues available through the Internet.

Nicholas Carolan
Irish Traditional Music Archive, Dublin
February 1997

It will be clear to readers that I would welcome further information on Francis O'Neill, and especially any information on his missing correspondence and music manuscripts.

INDEX

Balfe, William Michael 46
Bantry 5-7
Breathnach, Breandán 52, 56
Carolan, Turlough 39
Carthy, Tom 50
Chicago 9-11ff.
Chicago police 12-14
Chicago Gaelic Feis 51
Coleman, Michael 57
Cork Pipers' Club 26, 58-9
Cronin, Edward 35, 37, 46
Daly, Jerry 5, 25
Delaney, Bernard (Barney) 21, 27, 37-8
Downing, Timothy 7, 26
Dunn, Michael J. 50
Early, James 37, 52
Ennis, John & Tom 40-1
Fielding, Fr James 25, 37, 53
Gaelic League 7-8, 36
Gaynor, Fr Edward 45-6
Graves, Alfred Perceval 26
Great Famine 5
Hagerty, Peter (*An Píobaire Bán*) 7, 24
Hanafin, William & Michael 38
Henebry, Rev. Dr Richard 29, 35, 45
Hyde, Douglas 7
Irish language 7-8
Irish Music Club, Chicago 38-40
Kenny, Mrs Bridget 39, 61
McFadden, John 22, 37
McSweeney, Turlough 33
Murphy, Charley (*Cormac na bPaidreacha*) 7
Murphy, Paddy 56-7
O'Connor, Máirtín 58
O'Donovan Rossa, Jeremiah 6
O'Neill, Francis
- introduction 3
- origins and family 5, 25
- musical background 5-7
- Irish language ability 7-8
- music performance 7, 29-33, 52-3
- school life 8
- life at sea 9
- visits to Ireland 9, 25-6

- in America 9
- in Chicago 9ff.
- police life 10, 14-22
- police work and music 14, 20-2, 32-3
- character 23-5
- life after retirement 25-8, 46-53
- music collecting 26, 30-52
- personal library 28, 33, 52, 60
- death 28
- music literacy 35, 43
- editing procedures 40-3
- music publications
O'Neill's Music of Ireland 44-6, 51
The Dance Music of Ireland 46, 51
O'Neill's Irish Music. 250 Choice Selections...
46-7, 51
Irish Folk Music. A Fascinating Hobby 47, 49
Popular Selections from O'Neill's Dance Music of Ireland 49
Irish Minstrels and Musicians 49-51
O'Neill's Irish Music. 400 Choice Selections... 51
Waifs and Strays of Gaelic Melody (1st ed.) 51-2
Waifs and Strays of Gaelic Melody (2nd ed.) 52-3
articles 53
- motivations 53-4
- influence and importance 54-8, 60
O'Neill, James 22, 33-4, 37, 40-7
O'Neill, Rogers 25, 40
O'Neill, Selena 48-52
Ó Riabhaigh, Micheál 58-9
Piano arrangements 46-9, 51-2
Reavy, Ed 53, 56
Rogers, Anna (Mrs O'Neill) 9, 25, 28
Ryan's Mammoth Collection 44
Scottish music 33, 52
Shannon, Joe 53
Sullivan, A.M. & T.D. 6
Touhey, Patsy 37, 48, 61
Tralibane, Caheragh 5, 7
Walsh, Liam 58
Wayland, John Smithwick 26, 61
West, George 33